THE ADHD FOCUS FRIEND

Unhook from
self-shaming narratives
and partner with
your creative,
inconsistent, brilliant
ADHD brain.

The ADHD Focus Friend

A PLANNING + PRODUCTIVITY WORKBOOK

Grace Koelma

A TARCHERPERIGEE BOOK

tarcherperigee

an imprint of Penguin Random House LLC
penguinrandomhouse.com

Copyright © 2025 by Future ADHD Pty Ltd
10 Types of Rest reproduced with permission from Nicola Jane Hobbs.
Thanks to Bernice Li, Tara Breuso, Georgina Heslewood and Morgan Freney for contributing your stories.
Penguin Random House supports copyright. Copyright fuels creativity, encourages diverse voices, promotes free speech, and creates a vibrant culture. Thank you for buying an authorized edition of this book and for complying with copyright laws by not reproducing, scanning, or distributing any part of it in any form without permission. You are supporting writers and allowing Penguin Random House to continue to publish books for every reader.

TarcherPerigee with tp colophon is a registered trademark of Penguin Random House LLC.

Most TarcherPerigee books are available at special quantity discounts for bulk purchase for sales promotions, premiums, fundraising, and educational needs. Special books or book excerpts also can be created to fit specific needs. For details, write SpecialMarkets@penguinrandomhouse.com.

ISBN 9780593718681 (trade paperback)
ISBN 9780593853108 (ebook)

Printed in China
1 3 5 7 9 10 8 6 4 2

Interior layout by Grace Koelma
Interior design by Ali Rutten / Stoked Spruce Design Studio
Full page illustrations by Andrea Oerter
Supplementary illustrations by Huza Studio
Sticker art by Candice Cameron & Grace Koelma

To young me—one day you'll see that your "faults" are actually your best bits.

CONTENTS

Need help?
start on page 14 . . .

The Daily Focus Friend · 123

The Template Toolbox · 213

Foreword

Mariane Power, MPsych (Clin)

I'd just stepped off the stage after presenting a keynote on the brilliance and untapped potential of neurodivergent youth when Mikaela Koelma—a fellow female founder—bounced over to me. "You have to meet my sister-in-law, Grace. She's also an ADHD educator, and she's created this brilliant planner for ADHD people. You're going to love it!"

Having been diagnosed with ADHD only two years prior, I was keen to connect with women who, like me, had received a late diagnosis. I enthusiastically accepted Mikaela's kind offer of introduction.

The planner, on the other hand? That, I thought, I could give or take. Over the years, diaries and calendars had inevitably become dust collectors on my shelves. It seemed my messy mind was not suited to the typical structure of a time-bound, date-driven diary, its blank boxes a sign of my daily forgetfulness. If there's one thing I've come to understand about myself post-diagnosis, it's that I don't just think outside the box, I live outside it too. Nonetheless, I was intrigued how an ADHDer could actually stick to a planner, let alone create one.

Some weeks later, Grace dropped into my DMs, and we got chatting. From our first conversation, I was amazed by the depth of her knowledge about ADHD and neurodiversity. In the ultimate geek-fest, we laughed as we swapped research findings on how ADHDers can best navigate goal setting, organization, time, demand avoidance, autonomy and rejection sensitivity.

Eventually, my curiosity and FOMO got the better of me. I knew I had to explore whether an evidence-based ADHD planner would work for me. I'm pleased to share that rather than collecting dust, the Future ADHD planner is the first planner I've stuck with, because it really is designed for inconsistent ADHD brains.

I've created pages and pages of scribbles and colorings that sustain my focus in long meetings and phone calls, and added episode links to the thousands of podcasts I'm yet to listen to but have bookmarked with passion.

That's why I was so excited when Grace shared she was writing this book, *The ADHD Focus Friend*. Grace has combined some of the most popular templates from the Future ADHD planner with a deep dive into the inner workings of the ADHD brain. Underlying the success of Grace's work, I believe, is her ability to translate complex scientific findings and neurodivergent insights through the power of story, paired with bite-sized tips that keep our interest-based nervous systems coming back for more.

Like the Future ADHD planner, this book has captured my fears, hopes, dreams and heart, and to this day, remains my number-one dopamine delight personally, and my favorite resource recommendation for ADHDers professionally.

It's a gift when a big-hearted human dances on the earth at a time where their life experience, professional skills and eagerness to learn collide with a global need waiting to be met. Grace has dedicated her time to sift through cutting-edge research and lived-experience stories to ensure that evidence-based, practical strategies can reach you, no matter where you are in the world.

In my work as a clinical psychologist and certified ADHD coach, I've supported thousands of individuals globally, and I'm confident The ADHD Focus Friend will serve two needs for you. First, it will help you understand, radically accept and celebrate all parts of yourself, including the challenges and strengths that come with ADHD. Second, it will provide you with a space to discover, develop and deliver your unique potential to create a positive impact, whatever that looks like for you.

Research shows that ADHDers exhibit unique strengths, including cognitive dynamism, courage, energy, humanity, resilience and transcendence. These are the strengths required to imagine and design solutions that will heal our planet and all that inhabit it. And those strengths are within you, my friend. We're living at a point in time when the world needs your divergent thinking and bold action taking. That's why I'm so pleased you've picked up this book, and can't wait to witness the magic it helps you to create.

Mariane Power

Clinical Pyschologist + ADHD Coach, CEO of Posify

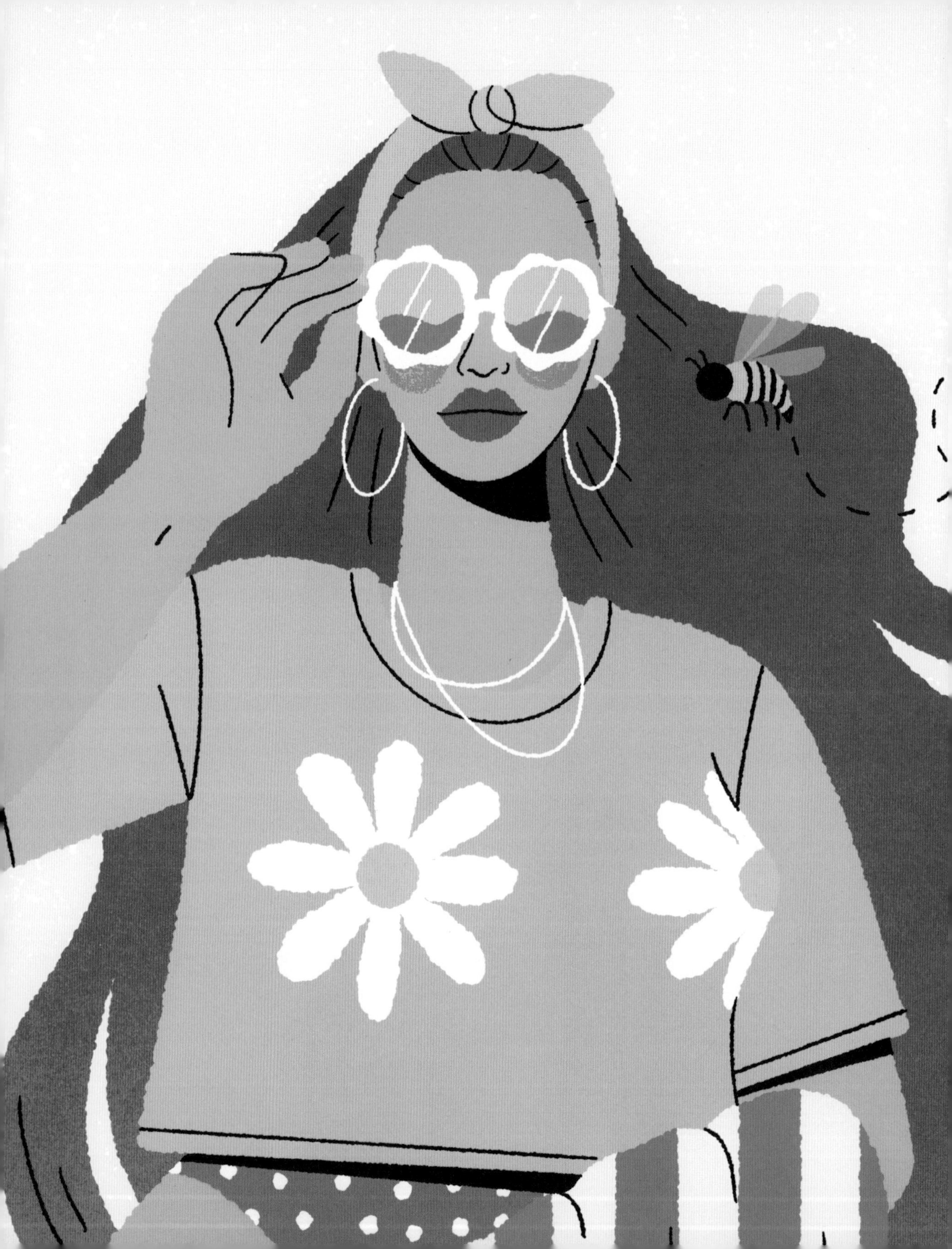

Introduction

Hi—I'm Grace. I was diagnosed with ADHD at the age of 33, but I've had a "neurospicy" brain my whole life. I vividly remember the exact moment I realized I had ADHD. I was researching it for my son, and somehow ended up reading an article about ADHD in adults. As I read the description of what ADHD felt like in the brain, suddenly everything clicked into place. It was as if I was finally seeing every moment of my life in high definition.

In the weeks that followed, I felt a mix of grief and relief. Relief that finally I had the words to describe how my brain worked, and grief as I ruminated on what could have been, had I known sooner. I began researching and writing about ADHD in order to make sense of my messy, too-fast thoughts, and explain what I was learning. I believe that more than anything, ADHDers want to be understood—by others and ourselves. We want to come home to ourselves, and ease into self-acceptance like collapsing on the couch at the end of a long day. This book is my invitation to continue your journey of self-understanding.

To live with an ADHD brain is to live with extremes in intensity of emotion, constant stimulation needs and crippling rejection sensitive dysphoria (RSD). It's to experience thoughts hurling themselves at us so thick and fast that we freeze—sometimes for hours, sometimes for weeks. It's the #ADHDtax. It's executive dysfunction that, at times, prevents us from leaving the house, cleaning or cooking meals.

It's over-committing to everything because we want to be everywhere at once, and then canceling at the last minute and maybe losing friends. It's sending a spicy text impulsively while doing 10 other things, then scouring text messages late at night, gripped by waves of RSD and regret. It's the long list of projects we started but couldn't finish. It's the sleep deprivation, the sensory overload and the procrastination cycles. **And yet . . .**

To live with ADHD is also to be a critical thinker, creative problem solver and incredible visionary. It's being passionate and eclectic in our tastes. For some ADHDers, it's doing the crazy, audacious thing other people tell us can't be done. For others, it's being open-minded and curious. It's noticing all of the tiny details on a nature walk, or being so deeply immersed in a good conversation that we barely notice the three Great Danes we almost tripped over.

It's the courage to take risks that sometimes pay off magnificently. Being ready for a spontaneous adventure and wanting to experience life in vivid color. Starting a business or learning a language rapidly by hyperfocusing on it. It's the ability to hold space and really witness people. It's the tendency to ask why, and be motivated by curiosity to keep learning. It's our deep need for authenticity and self-expression.

In a world that defines ADHD only in terms of its deficits, I prefer to begin conversations on ADHD by defining myself by who I <u>am</u>, instead of what I'm <u>not</u>.

You make sense.

This isn't to dismiss the very real challenges that come with being neurodivergent in a world that wasn't designed for our brains. Executive dysfunction and emotional dysregulation have very real consequences, including job loss, mental health struggles, addiction, relationship breakdown and self-harm.

But I've noticed that my biggest ADHD deficit isn't the sleep deprivation, demand avoidance or even the anxiety. It's the shame I've carried with me since childhood. It's the basic, unspoken fear in a question: "What's wrong with me?"

Know this. There is nothing wrong with you. Your brain makes sense.

I don't know your story and your experience with ADHD, but I can guess it's likely marked by sleepless nights, and understandable frustration, epiphanies, confusion and anger. You have dreams and goals you want to pursue, but right now it seems like you'll never climb out from under the mountain of to-dos. And it feels unfair.

You wrestle with the cognitive dissonance of knowing you're talented, with so much to give, but worry if you can't even take yourself seriously, how will anyone else? You're frustrated at the times you get a random hit of dopamine and accomplish a huge amount in a short period of time, but then lose that motivation just as quickly, with very little to show for it. There's "potential" there, you think, but if nothing ever gets finished, what's the point?

These questions make sense, and they're justified. You probably want to give up, and I wouldn't blame you . . . but before you do, I hope you try this productivity workbook—one that's actually designed for your ADHD brain.

I lived more than 30 years without the context of ADHD to frame my lived experience. I tried out so many planners, but they never seemed to stick and always ended up collecting dust on my bedside table. Sound familiar? I thought I sucked at follow-through and felt like a disorganized failure most of the time, but now I know that most planners are designed for neurotypical brains—marked by their one-size-fits-all structure and rigidity. When I stopped trying to fit my square brain into a round hole, life exhaled.

The ADHD Focus Friend is designed to support your ADHD brain—full of inconsistency, passion and above all, possibility! As you flick through these pages, you'll continue your journey of self-discovery to learn how your brain thrives, seeks balance and makes sense of the world. .

Welcome to The ADHD Focus Friend.

Grace Koelma
Founder of Future ADHD

> You'll notice I reference scientific research and other statistics throughout this book. Check the Notes section (in the last few pages) for a list of citations.

How to use this book

This isn't your average ADHD productivity tool. It's part book, part undated planner. Maybe you want to learn more about why productivity is so closely tied to emotional regulation and the state of your nervous system? If so, start with Section 1. Perhaps you just want to sort the jumbled mess of to-do lists in your brain into something more organized and coherent? In that case, flick straight to The Daily Focus Friend in Section 2 (about halfway through).

Ultimately, I invite you to use this book for what you need in this season—not what you think you "should" be doing. Inconsistency is perfectly acceptable here. It's okay to use **The ADHD Focus Friend** for a few days, put it down for two weeks and then pick it up again. Just like a real friend, it will be here waiting for you. That's why this isn't a typical "planner" (as you'll soon find out).

As you go, feel free to highlight the sections that you want to revisit, write your reflections in the Your Thoughts journal prompts or doodle in the corners when your mind wanders. Yes, I know that might feel weird, but remember you don't ruin the book by writing in it. You make it **whole.**

Section 1 covers the strengths and challenges of ADHD, with chapters on emotional regulation, the nervous system and goal setting. You'll be guided through my theories (as well as the findings of many other experts and evidence-based studies) on what truly makes ADHDers tick and how this affects our productivity. Using a timer and checklist can be great, but this book will show you that being **aligned with who you are and what you need** on a physiological level will trump any productivity hack out there.

Section 2 is where you put theory into practice. It contains a ton of undated daily pages and a resource template library called the Template Toolbox. This section is a loving home for all your random thoughts, to-dos, projects and goals—big or small. Here you'll find templates that are intuitive to your ADHD needs and provide a refuge in the storm of life, so you can work out what your next steps should be and what you can let go of. These templates are guilt-free—go at your own pace, and find your rhythm.

So throw on your comfy pants, grab a crunchy snack (for dopamine!) and let's put pen to paper! You can use this box for testing out your fave highlighters and pens.

Ready to dive in?

Check out page 18 . . .

Just found out you have ADHD? Are you feeling confused and alone?

Go to page 43 . . .

Want to make today feel a little bit more organized than yesterday?

Always running late and forgetting things? Dirty dishes staring at you?

Flip to page 123 . . .

Jump to page 81 . . .

Want to learn what to do when self-care is stressful?

Stuck thinking about all the possibilities and need to make a decision?

Got a million things in your brain and don't want to forget them?

Explore page 127 . . .

Check out page 120 . . .

Start at page 213 . . .

Want to celebrate your wins, small or big? Looking for "glimmers" in your day?

Head to page 32 . . .

Head to page 102 . . .

Can't get off the couch? Feel like you're stuck in a procrastination cycle?

Feeling frazzled? Are the lights too bright or is that background noise annoying you?

Feeling like you'll never measure up or "get it together"?

Read page 72 . . .

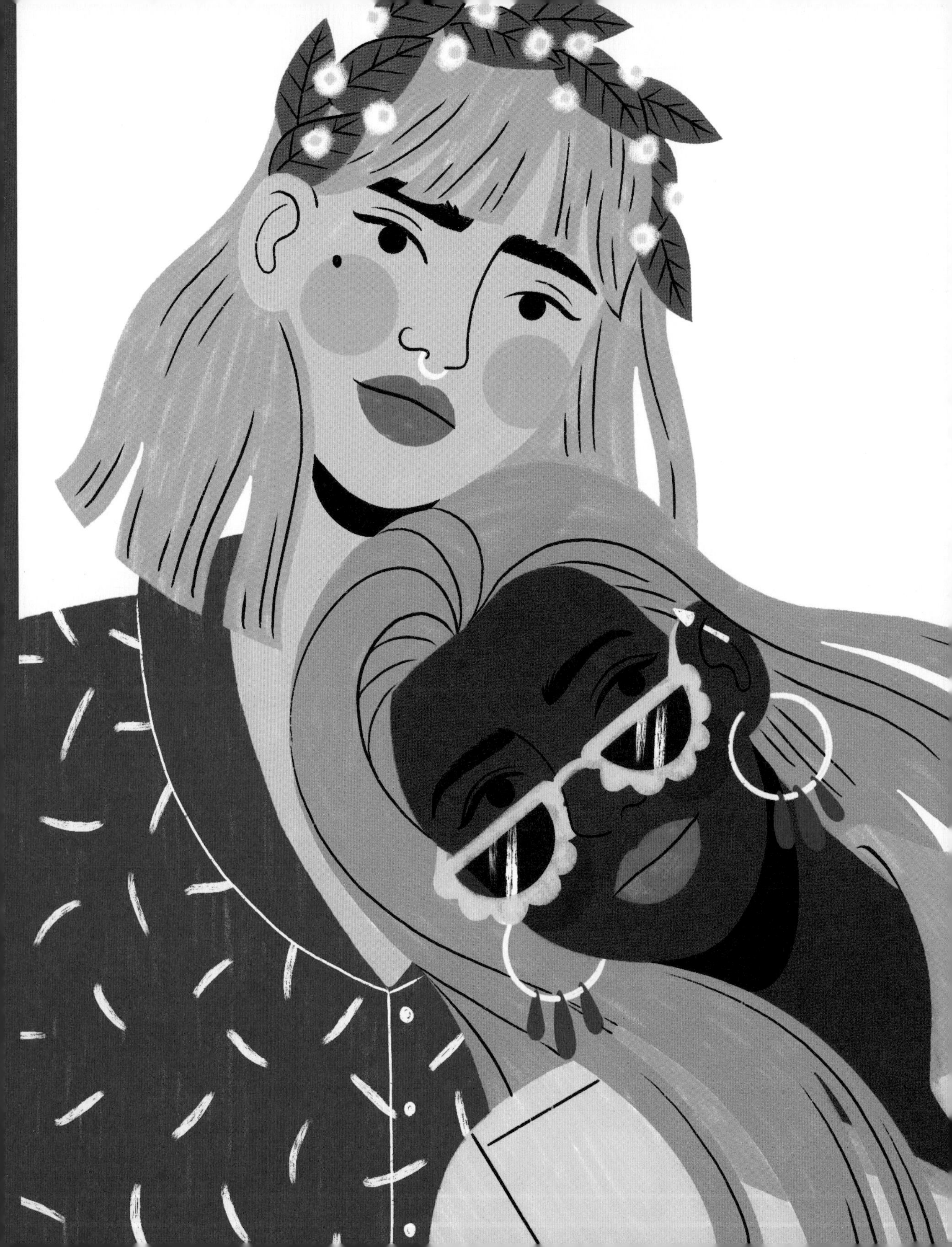

ADHD
Explained

Whether you're self-diagnosed, late-diagnosed or are just exploring whether you have ADHD, this is an invitation to learn more about yourself. When we read about the _why_ behind our complex set of traits and behaviors, paired with recent discoveries in ADHD research, we feel less alone. We can better understand our triggers and patterns and take pride in our ADHD brain and the strengths it gives us. Starting with curiosity instead of judgement helps us crack open the door to let acceptance and self-permission flow in like a breath of fresh air. Are you ready?

The ADHD basics

What is ADHD?

Attention-deficit/hyperactivity disorder (ADHD) is a multifaceted neurobiological condition that tends to run in families. It occurs in an estimated 5.9 percent of children and 2.5 percent of adults. People may describe themselves as ADHDers, neurodivergent, neurospicy or as having an ADHD brain. ADHD can show up in lots of ways, and traits vary from person to person.

Three "types" of ADHD

According to the *DSM-5* (the diagnostic manual used by doctors globally), ADHD is split into **three** separate presentations:

In earlier versions of the DSM, ADHD was referred to as ADD.

- **Hyperactive-Impulsive ADHD**
- **Inattentive ADHD**
- **Combined ADHD**

See the Notes section for page-specific sources.

Hyperactive-Impulsive ADHD

People with Hyperactive-Impulsive ADHD may feel driven as if by a motor, have difficulty sitting still or waiting, make impulsive decisions, overspend, interrupt frequently and change moods unexpectedly. They're also usually passionate, stubborn, uncannily intuitive, fun, adventurous and cool-headed in a crisis. They experience intensity, excessive restlessness, difficulty winding down and mental hyperactivity resulting in "stimming" (self-stimulating behaviors like tapping, twirling hair or biting nails).

Inattentive ADHD

People with Inattentive ADHD tend to be forgetful, distracted and disorganized, prone to emotional mood swings and experience time differently (time blindness). They're often deep thinkers and visionaries, with a constant stream of ideas, and a great deal of creativity, emotional sensitivity and empathy. In many cases Inattentive ADHDers can suffer from analysis paralysis and lower activity, rather than hyperactivity. Often, those with Inattentive ADHD get called "lazy" and may struggle with low self-esteem.

Combined ADHD

People with a combined presentation of ADHD have traits across both the Hyperactive-Impulsive and Inattentive domains. I have combined-type ADHD.

Regardless of the type, it's important to know that ADHD expresses itself differently in everyone!

Formal ADHD diagnosis

To get a formal ADHD diagnosis, you'll need to see a psychiatrist or psychologist, who will perform a detailed assessment of your personal, work and childhood experiences and determine whether you meet clinical criteria for ADHD according to the DSM-5. To establish whether you experienced ADHD symptoms in childhood, you may need to supply records, such as school reports. A diagnosis may be validating, help you find support and give you access to ADHD medication and neurodivergent workplace accommodations.

Self-diagnosis

Self-diagnosis is linked to a deep understanding of self; you identify with the label and characteristics of ADHD, but you're either on a waitlist for diagnosis, have chosen not to pursue a diagnosis or are unable to receive a diagnosis due to cost or accessibility factors. Self-diagnosis can help you find self-validation, support and better strategies. Feeling seen and validated can help you feel less lonely and grow to accept yourself more. It can also offer you access to broader social and global communities who understand you. It's important to note that without a medical diagnosis, you won't have access to ADHD medication.

The emotional journey of a late ADHD diagnosis

If you've been diagnosed with ADHD as an adult and are trying to make sense of your childhood and huge portions of your adult life, you're not alone. Studies have consistently shown that females are under-diagnosed in childhood; however, there is little research looking at the impact of this under-diagnosis. What we do know is that ADHD is more commonly diagnosed in males because:

- health providers are less informed about how girls and women present with ADHD
- many symptoms are internalized for females and externalized for males
- due to a strong desire to fit in and an ability to observe and copy others, many ADHD girls hide their ADHD symptoms (a strategy known as "masking") to avoid social rejection or getting into trouble

If you've been **diagnosed or self-diagnosed late in life**, know that it's normal to feel a range of emotions—**maybe grief, anger or regret** over the difficulties and missed opportunities you've faced due to undiagnosed ADHD. There can be a lot of shame too, as you reflect on the negative comments you've received across your life from parents, friends, romantic partners and teachers. You may also feel **relief** that you now have an explanation for your struggles and you're not "lazy" or a "failure." Listening to podcasts where adults talk about their experience being diagnosed late can help. Remember that you don't have to fix everything today—awareness is such a huge first step, so be patient and give yourself time to process.

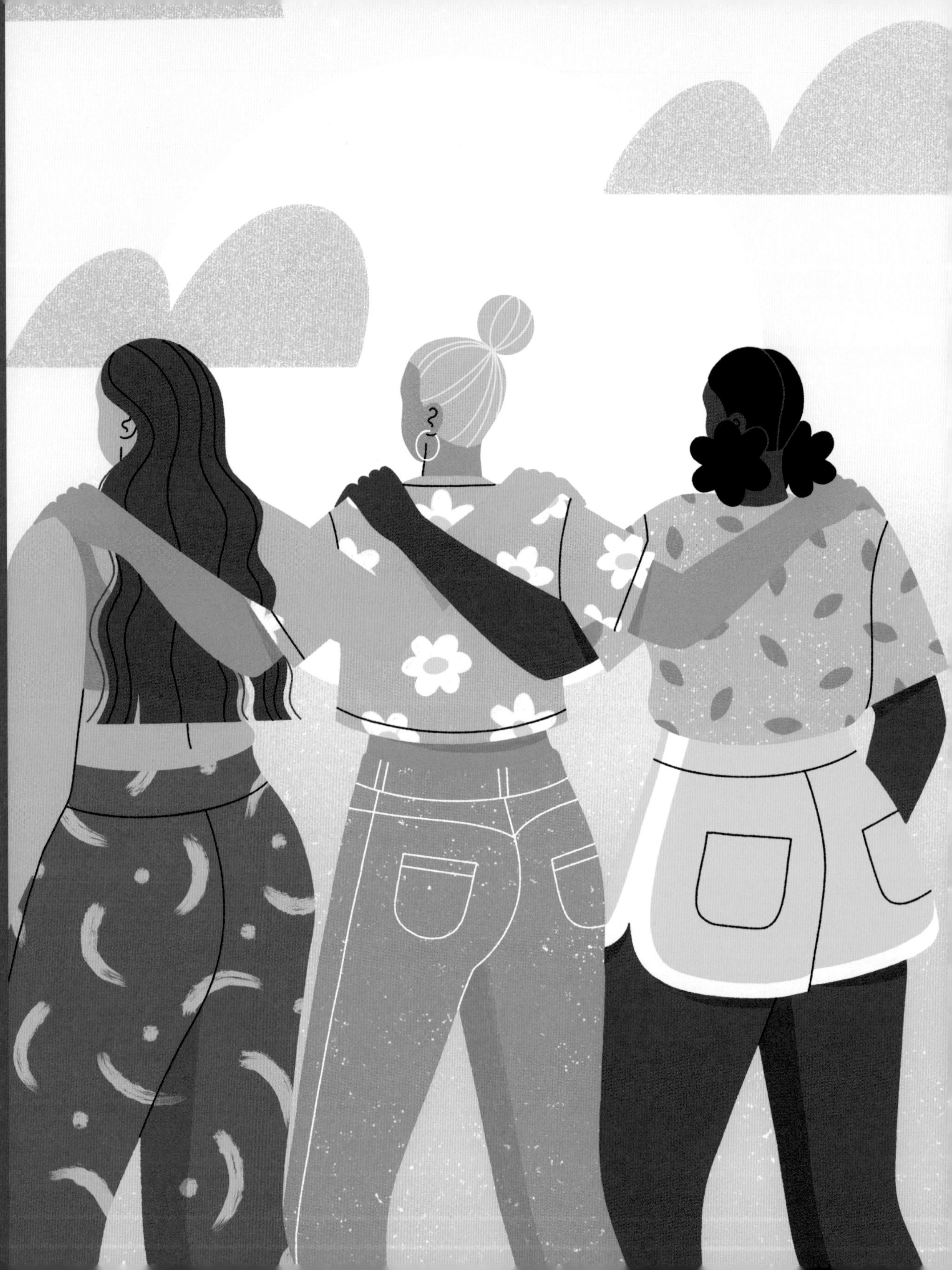

Intersectionality

ADHD is often discussed as if it were a static, defined neurobiological condition. But in reality, experiences of neurodiversity are messy, layered and influenced by a range of socio-economic factors. Intersectionality is a way of understanding how different aspects of a person's identity all come together to influence their experiences and the challenges they may face.

Factors that impact your experience of ADHD include (but aren't limited to):

- where you were born
- your gender identity and sexuality
- your race
- access to education
- your upbringing and family dynamic
- wealth and security
- history of abuse and/or trauma
- where you live and access to healthcare providers
- comorbid mental health conditions or disabilities
- caring for neurodivergent children or children with other support needs
- caring for aging parents or other dependents
- access to a supportive community/a supportive partner

These added layers of intersectionality magnify discrimination and marginalization for neurodivergent people.

If you are a Black, single ADHD mother raising children who also have ADHD, your experience will vary hugely from a straight, middle-class white entrepreneur with ADHD, which will be very different from a queer 15-year-old girl with ADHD.

Living with ADHD (and a complex array of other vulnerablities) in a world that isn't designed for neurodivergents isn't easy. While I take an inherently strengths-based approach to ADHD, I recognize that the ability to see the "gifts" of ADHD is a privilege. While not everyone has access to an environment that will champion their neurodiversity as a strength, it remains true that **every single human deserves to feel seen, safe and supported—in school, families, work settings and society in general.** Little by little, let's work towards a world like that.

No matter what your story is, this book offers you a safe place where your brain makes sense—a way to reframe your struggles, un-shame your past and learn to work with your ADHD brain.

The strength of neurodiversity

"Neurodiversity" is a term embraced by the neurodivergent community as a source of pride and celebration. The concept of neurodiversity is often attributed to autistic Australian sociologist Judy Singer, who coined the term in the 1990s to destigmatize the inherent range of brain differences within the human population.

Nobel Prize-winning biologist Gerald Edelman viewed the human brain uniquely, likening the brain to an "individual rainforest, filled with growth, change, competition, variety, and selection." Thomas Armstrong, PhD, said that the diversity among brains is as enriching as biodiversity and the diversity among cultures and races.

The common thread among these voices and experts is that our society becomes more resilient when we acknowledge, respect and appreciate the extensive spectrum of neurodiversity among humans. When everyone flourishes, we're stronger. Recent studies have investigated societal attitudes and the stigma surrounding ADHD, which have arisen from a medical model primarily focused on deficits. The general consensus is that we need a shift towards emphasizing the diversity of ADHD experiences and celebrating ADHD strengths.

ADHD is a spectrum

ADHD is often associated with a single stereotype—loud, disruptive, restless and disorganized. However, ADHD actually encompasses a wide spectrum of traits. Many of these traits (forgetfulness, mood swings, addictive tendencies, fidgeting) are experiences shared by most people at various times, which can make it confusing. But really, ADHD is measured by the severity and frequency of these traits; essentially, how much they affect your daily life. ADHD is not a one-size-fits-all condition. You'll experience your neurodivergence differently from your ADHD friend. It's a complex interplay of traits impacting your life, which is why diagnosis and treatment need to be tailored to each person.

Comorbidities with ADHD

"Comorbidity" refers to the presence of two or more medical conditions or disorders in an individual at the same time. These conditions can either exist independently or interact with each other, influencing the course of both. ADHD is often accompanied by a range of comorbidities.

For example, ADHD is linked to a significantly higher lifetime risk of major depression, multiple anxiety disorders, bipolar disorder, autism, learning disorders like dyslexia and dyspraxia, oppositional-defiant disorder and Tourette's/tic disorders. It's also correlated with significantly higher risk of insomnia, substance abuse, chronic pain and suicidal ideation. These risks reduce when neurodivergents have access to supports, community, medication and therapy.

ADHD challenges

These are some of the very real challenges ADHDers can face that impact significantly on productivity, goal setting, relationships, jobs and wellness. Many of these skills are crucial for functioning in school and later as a responsible adult. We need extra support in these areas.

Impulsive/risk-taking

Executive dysfunction

Time blindness

Distractible/forgetful

Color in or highlight the areas that resonate for you.

Analysis paralysis

Chronic procrastination

Rejection sensitivity

Disorganized

Trouble winding down

Impatient

Sudden intense emotions

Daydreaming

Easily bored/restless

Demand avoidance

Difficulty following through

Anxiety/depression

Low self-esteem

Oversharing

ADHD strengths

These traits are based on the work of strengths-focused ADHD experts like Dr. Edward Hallowell, Dr. John Ratey and Dr. William Dodson. Many of these qualities are dependent on our interest-based nervous system, and tend to show up when we're fascinated by something.

Creative problem-solving

Passionate + idealistic

Irrepressible curiosity

Life enthusiast

Divergent, prolific ideas

Big-picture thinking

Lifelong learner

Check back in after reading and see if you can add any more.

Courage to speak out

Spontaneous + offbeat

Attention to detail

Insightful + intuitive

Advocate for others

Exuberant + joyful

Sensitive + thoughtful

Original + innovative

Tenacious + persistent

Generous + big-hearted

Deeply focused

Life with an ADHD brain can feel very lonely at times. No matter what your story is, this book offers you a safe place where your brain makes sense—a way to reframe your struggles, un-shame your past and learn to work with your ADHD brain.

Your thoughts

Reflect on your journey so far and the whirlwind of emotions that may have come up for you (perhaps grief, relief, insight, anger, resentment or regret). Naming each feeling and writing it down helps untangle the big ball of intense feelings a little.

Finding a community of people who love you for who you are is so important. Write down the people you have shared (or want to share) your ADHD diagnosis journey with. Make a note to find some online social media groups for ADHDers too.

ADHD in women

The past four decades of research on women and ADHD has shown that women and girls experience ADHD very differently from men and boys.

Early research studies primarily focused on the more noticeable ADHD traits typically associated with boys, such as hyperactivity and impulsivity. As a result, many girls with ADHD whose symptoms were not as overt or disruptive were often overlooked or misdiagnosed.

It's important to mention that very few scientific studies have focused on ADHD gender nonconforming or genderqueer individuals and trans women with ADHD, which I hope will change in the future. An understanding of how people of all genders experience neurodivergence is crucial in learning more about neurodiversity.

The pain of being misunderstood

Recent studies indicate that because of misinformation and societal stigmas, women with ADHD face a range of challenging issues beyond the common symptoms of hyperactivity, impulsivity and inattention. **Can you relate to these examples?**

Perhaps you were bullied in school, or went through childhood facing confusion, self-blame, rejection and the hurt of not being understood or appreciated by others.	Doing "simple" household tasks and chores may be challenging for you, and it might trigger feelings of shame and embarrassment when friends come over to visit.
Memories of difficult times during your childhood or instances when your ADHD affected you negatively can lead to decreased self-esteem and less confidence in your capabilities.	You could struggle with picking up on social cues, feel awkward in social situations and accidentally say things that offend, which might make it tough in social or work environments.
You might often deal with negative thoughts like "What's wrong with me," "I'm a failure" and "I hate myself," and these thoughts could lead to overthinking and analysis paralysis.	You may also experience strong bursts of anger. You realize you're overreacting, but you find it difficult to control those emotions and don't know why.

Relationships

ADHD can bring real challenges to relationships. Picture this: You're in the middle of a heartfelt conversation, and suddenly your mind takes off on a wild tangent, leaving your partner or friend hanging. Or the forgetfulness hits, and you're left explaining why you missed your friend's brunch–again. ADHDers are also prone to snap decisions or emotionally charged reactions that can bewilder their friends or partner. It's like being caught on a roller coaster of intense feelings that are hard to predict or handle.

Hormonal changes

Hormonal fluctuations during menstruation, pregnancy and menopause can intensify ADHD symptoms for women, leading to heightened difficulties with focus, organization and emotional regulation. These hormonal shifts might exacerbate the existing struggles that ADHD women face in managing their daily responsibilities. This can result in increased forgetfulness, impulsivity, stress, mood swings and heightened emotional sensitivity.

Pregnancy and motherhood

Women who have been able to "mask" ADHD for many years will often become overwhelmed if they become mothers, and find they experience more executive dysfunction (a breakdown in one's capacity to manage and coordinate higher-level cognitive processes, including planning, decision-making and organization). Even with a supportive partner, factors like sleep deprivation, the sensory overload of screaming children, managing overlapping schedules, cleaning the house, getting meals on the table and reduced personal time all impact hugely on self-regulation (see page 89 for more on this). Impulsivity and forgetting to use contraception have an impact too. Studies show that the rates of unplanned pregnancy and teen motherhood are up to five times higher in women with ADHD.

Work and study

Women with ADHD often face complex obstacles in work and education. Attention issues and emotional dysregulation frequently result in errors and inconsistency, while problems with organization and procrastination lead to missed deadlines. Executive functioning difficulties make tasks overwhelming, and sensory sensitivity only adds to the challenge in noisy workplaces or study environments. These struggles are made more stressful because there isn't yet a culture or common language for women to describe these difficulties, and they can end up feeling gaslit, or gaslighting themselves. Although you may feel confident in your ADHD diagnosis while sitting in your psychiatrist's office, when you have to advocate for your needs, self-doubt creeps in, and you begin to wonder if you're just lazy or hopelessly disorganized. Stigma and the fear of disclosure also play significant roles; some women worry that sharing their ADHD diagnosis with their boss or colleagues may result in being judged as incompetent, potentially leading to inadequate support or an unfair job loss.

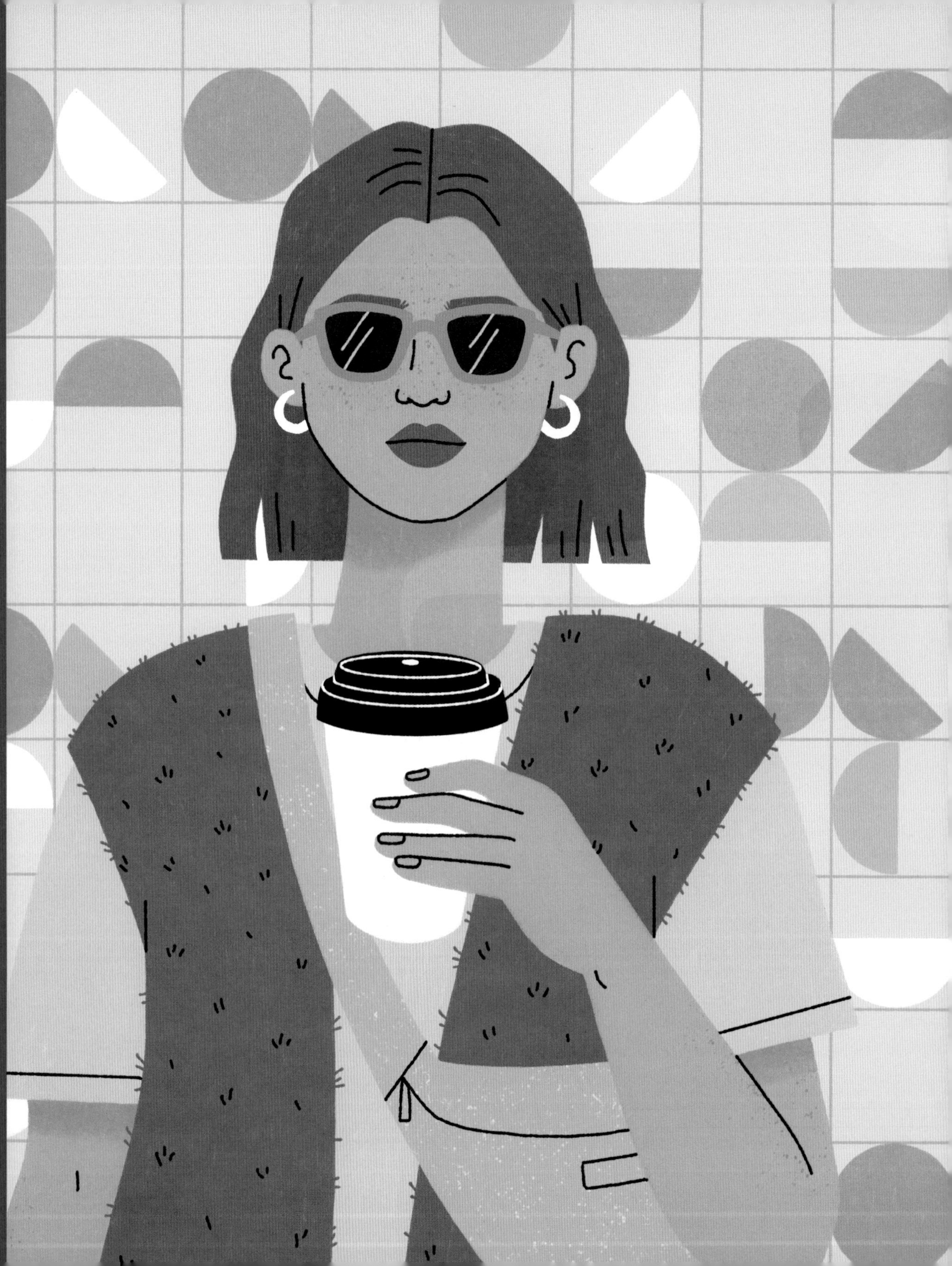

ADHD masking

"Masking" is essentially covering up your ADHD traits in an attempt to fit in and be "normal" in a society that often expects us to be organized, attentive and calm. While masking affects almost everyone with ADHD to an extent, women are conditioned to mask from a young age. According to psychotherapist Sari Solden, ADHD girls typically learn which types of learning and social styles are embraced or tolerated and which ones are looked down upon. This is why girls able to fly under the radar and often go undiagnosed until later in life.

Masking could look like:

- hiding hyperactivity with calmness (or stimming subtly)
- having to come up with excuses why you're late or distracted
- rushing to tidy your house a minute before a friend comes by
- pretending to enjoy a friend's party when you're actually overstimulated
- participating in class or work discussions appropriately, even when your thoughts are all over the place
- hiding your big emotions from your kids
- chitchatting politely when you just want to be direct and get the job done

---

Masking can be a useful social strategy, helping ADHDers maintain friendships and important work relationships, but it takes a heavy toll. Masking is exhausting, meaning we have less energy to invest in relationships, hobbies or self-care. Masking can also lead to internal conflict, where we work tirelessly to maintain an outward appearance that does not align with our true internal experiences. Masking can be very draining, particularly if we don't have many (or any) places or safe relationships where we can "drop the mask" and just be ourselves. Studies on emotional regulation have also shown that repressing emotions by masking activates the stress response in our nervous system.

Your thoughts

Which situations do you mask in the most, and how does that impact your energy?

Low self-esteem

There is a strong link between ADHD and low self-esteem. Research shows that people of all ages with ADHD (specifically untreated ADHD) struggle with notably low self-esteem compared to their non-ADHD peers, but this is particularly prevalent in women. Feeling bad about ourselves directly influences and reduces our executive functioning, social skills and emotional regulation. I think of the cycle like this:

We lack confidence
in our abilities

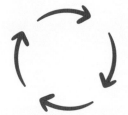

We are more error-prone
and forgetful

We develop a low
self-esteem

We make mistakes & feel
worse about ourselves

How the self-doubt cycle affects us

Our low self-esteem may mean we have a harder time believing in our own capabilities, and this lack of confidence can actually worsen our ADHD symptoms. At school or work, you might feel like you're lagging behind. You miss deadlines, your projects are a mess and it seems like everyone else has it all together. It's easy to think, "Maybe I'm just not cut out for this."

Friends or family may point out our mistakes, and it's as if they're saying, "Hey, you missed the memo on how to adult." We've got a backpack full of "not measuring up" labels, and it's getting heavier by the day. And the kicker—when we're doubting ourselves, it's even tougher to concentrate on tasks, stay on top of to-dos and keep those impulsive thoughts in check.

Then there's the endless comparisons—your friends are breezing through tasks you find incredibly challenging. It's like they're playing on beginner while you're stuck on hard mode. It's not a competition, but that doesn't stop the feeling of falling short.

People with ADHD can achieve incredible success. But because we often feel like a hot mess in so many other parts of our life, we (or other people) can dismiss our success and put it down to fluke or luck, which makes the self-doubt cycle intensify. Fighting against this imposter syndrome is exhausting.

Shame in childhood

Researcher Dr. William Dodson estimates that *children with ADHD receive an astounding 20,000 more negative or corrective messages by the age of 12 than their non-ADHD peers.*

Children are incredibly sensitive to the messages they receive from their environment, particularly from authority figures like parents, teachers and peers. When these messages are mostly disparaging, it deteriorates their self-perception and well-being.

Dr. Emily Anhalt is a clinical psychologist who spent two years conducting qualitative research on successful adults with ADHD. She found the most painful part of each person's story wasn't about dealing with the symptoms of ADHD but "with the feelings of incompetence, loneliness and shame that they had about themselves."

The sheer volume of thoughts and our tendency to overthink means ADHDers can get stuck in a **rumination loop**, overthinking and hyperfocusing on our struggles. The futility we feel saps our energy and robs us of essential skills in executive functioning, logic and emotional regulation. In this book, I'll use a shame-free approach that helps you get some wins on the board to build self-trust and exit this rumination loop for good.

Your thoughts

Write about a time when feelings of inadequacy and failure stopped you from taking a risk, making a friend, going for that job or trying something new.

What is AuDHD?

"AuDHD" is a word representing people who identify as both ADHD and autistic. People who meet diagnostic criteria for both ADHD and autism usually prefer to use the term "AuDHD" (pronounced *aww-D-H-D*) instead of "ADHD" to describe themselves. #AuDHD is also used as a search term and hashtag on social media to help people find their community and educational resources.

There are many layers of overlap between ADHD and autistic traits, and some significant differences. The website Neurodivergent Insights has some fantastic information, including a Venn diagram which I've adapted below. This is not a definitive guide, and there are many more nuances to explore in the interplay of autism and ADHD than this book has time to dedicate to. If you're interested in finding out more, please continue to do your own research.

ADHD

Seeks novelty

Hyperactive + impulsive

Missing social cues due to scattered attention

Regulation + focus issues

Inhibition difficulties

Autism

Seeks familiarity

Strict adherence to routines

Difficulty reading non-autistic social cues intuitively

Finds comfort in repetitive behaviors

High need for verbal context

(Overlap)

Stimming

Interoception issues

Sensory differences

Executive dysfunction

Rejection sensitivity

Special interests + passions

Impulse control issues

Task-switching difficulties

Neurodivergent masking

Passion + intensity

Hyperfocus ability

Oversharing

Morgan's story

ADHD AND AUTISM (AUDHD)

I was clinically diagnosed with (what was then called) Asperger's syndrome when I was 13, while my 10-year-old brother was diagnosed with ADHD. We've both always known we were on the same "brain wave frequency," but because of his obvious hyperactivity and impulsivity compared to my own symptoms, I never considered until recently that ADHD could present any differently. When I started reading about the science behind ADHD and autism for the first time, I realized ADHD often presents differently in women and girls, as we're conditioned to hide any flaws or differences.

After struggling extensively over the past four years maintaining focus during my PhD in biotechnology, I'm now in the process of being diagnosed with AuDHD (autism and ADHD). I find that I am particularly forgetful in the lab and put this down to "just" problems with memory, which I've had my whole life but have worsened as the complexity of my work increases.

Living with undiagnosed ADHD can be debilitating. It's easy for medical professionals to dismiss our struggles as mental illness rather than symptoms that arise from being a neurodivergent who lives life outside societal norms. Having a label can be beneficial because it allows you to put a finger on what the problem actually is and work on ways to address your dysregulation and bring it within your control, harnessing the way your mind works.

I find that people don't believe that I could struggle or suffer in any way with these symptoms due to my outward success.

My naturally hyperactive thoughts and mental impulsivity have become internalized ADHD, and this constant masking has led to long episodes of depression and dysregulation.

ADHD can be a gift and a curse, but I wouldn't want to change the way my brain is wired. My inner world is so complex, vibrant and detailed that it's often much more interesting and engaging than what's happening externally. My "inattention" is not really inattention but rather a preference for thinking about interesting subject matters. What is termed "daydreaming" is, for me, theorization and imagination. One day, I hope we can all acknowledge how neurodiversity is an incredible strength, on both an individual and a societal level.

" The inside of my mind is more intellectually stimulating than anything happening externally in my day-to-day life. "

Morgan

Dopamine motivated

Have you ever been accused of being lazy? Or muttered under your breath: *"It's not that hard, why am I so useless?"* ADHD has long been viewed from the lens of an attention deficit. But, like many ADHDers, I believe we have attention in abundance—it's channeling the attention that's the hard part. Enter a little neurotransmitter called dopamine . . .

Scientists are confident about the connection between dopamine and ADHD, largely because stimulant medication has been shown to be a highly effective treatment for ADHD. Simply put, prescription stimulants like dextroamphetamine and methylphenidate boost dopamine and norepinephrine stores in the brain, rapidly improving focus, motivation and emotional regulation in ADHDers. But while the link is clear, the complex nature of how dopamine pathways operate in the ADHD brain is still an emerging (and exciting) area of research.

Even so, neurodivergents often describe their lives as being "dopamine motivated"; whether it's bingeing salty snacks or hours spent online shopping, post-workout highs or vivid daydreams during work meetings, our search for dopamine seems constant, and heavily dictates our priorities. Have you noticed how spending 14 hours straight making cosplay wings out of EVA foam is as easy as breathing—and yet your laundry will sit wet in the basket (the "too-hard basket") for five to seven business days? Dopamine may seem to serve frivolous purposes, but there's more to this happy chemical than meets the eye.

Dopamine is a dark horse

It may be known for its hedonistic qualities, but I see dopamine as a "dark horse," playing a role in keeping our executive functioning in top shape. **Studies show dopamine is a key ingredient in motivation, learning and task completion.** Dopamine is part of a chemical cocktail that helps you make good decisions, set goals and learn from your mistakes.

- ✦ One broadly cited 2010 meta-analysis (a study summarizing the findings of many other studies) theorized that dopamine neurons have different roles because they don't send the same motivational signal to all brain areas. In imaging studies, some dopamine neurons responded with excitement to negative stimuli, and others did not.

- ✦ A 2018 research paper speculated that dopamine may even have the ability to switch between motivational and learning "modes," in response to what's needed.

- ✦ Numerous experiments have also shown that dopamine neurons get excited about larger rewards as opposed to smaller ones; more probable rewards compared to less likely ones; and immediate rewards rather than delayed ones. Fascinating, huh?

✳ **If dopamine is this crucial for executive functioning, finding healthy dopamine sources should be a priority. Flick to the next page for my "DopaMINE" ideas.**

DopaMINE rewards list

Bookmark these pages so you have a handy little dopamine menu to choose from. You'll find these reward suggestions helpful in the Daily Focus Friend section too—starting on page 123.

Unplug

- Be uncontactable for a night (turn off your phone and enjoy the silence)
- Do some earthing (simply standing on the grass with bare feet)
- Browse a bookstore at your own pace
- Buy a magazine (and actually sit down and read it)
- Do a long, slow lap around your garden (or down your street)
- Literally go and smell the roses
- Cuddle or play with your pet
- Spend time in your garden (or even gardening, if that feels relaxing to you)
- Try origami (watch YouTube tutorials)
- Do a crossword or suduko
- Paint
- Draw
- Do some woodworking
- Go to a museum or gallery

Something new

- Order something from your favorite restaurant that you've never tried before
- Go on a photography adventure
- Do something exhilarating (high ropes course, zip-lining, go-karting, skiing)
- Write your own fun list of things you would consider a reward for doing boring tasks
- Plan a vacation/trip
- Watch an interesting TED Talk

Get outside

- Go for a short walk
- Go for a hike
- Watch the birds
- Go for a bike ride
- Go stargazing
- Go for a swim (pool, lake, ocean)
- Spend five minutes in direct sunlight
- Jump in puddles
- Watch the sunset or sunrise
- Head to the beach
- Go for a skate
- Go to the park
- Hug a tree
- Sit under the tree instead
- Watch a thunderstorm
- Pick flowers

With friends

- Play a board game
- Call a friend
- Hang out with friends
- Play a video game with a friend
- Send a kind message to a friend
- Play with your kids
- Look up local events to attend (any upcoming festivals in your town? Maybe that could be your reward next time!)

 Circle some you'd like to try!

Old favorites

- Watch your favorite show
- Read that book you've been putting off
- Look through old photo albums
- Watch funny videos online (guilt free, you earned it)
- Order something delicious from your favorite restaurant
- Go to the movies
- Play a musical instrument
- Go retro, and watch an old movie, concert or TV show on DVD
- Sort through your wardrobe to find fun new combos (you've probably got stuff you rarely/never wear . . . ?)
- Learn how to use that thing you bought in a hyperfocus flurry and then never touched (I'm looking at you, DSLR camera)
- Play a favorite game on your phone (set a timer)

Tasty treats

- Have a cup of tea/coffee
- Enjoy a sweet treat
- Go to the local produce market
- Have a few sneaky bites of chocolate from the stash you hide from your kids!
- Have a picnic in your backyard
- Bake your grandma's famous recipe
- Eat your lunch in the sun
- Go to a restaurant
- Enjoy a savory snack

Low pressure

- Take a nap
- Do a sensory cocoon
- Do some light stretching
- Do a foot spa (feet in the bath or a bucket)
- Paint your nails
- Do a face mask
- Have a dance party
- Listen to binaural beats/brown noise
- Go to bed early
- Listen to a podcast
- Play with a "stimming" toy (fidget toys, modeling clay or a Rubik's Cube)
- Do a two-minute full-body scan meditation
- Sit in the comfiest chair in the house and just S.T.O.P. and rest for a bit
- Take a bath
- Realize that baths aren't always relaxing and take a shower instead
- Light a candle and just watch it burn
- Do some coloring
- Go to the gym
- Listen to an audiobook
- Play your favorite music

Add your own:

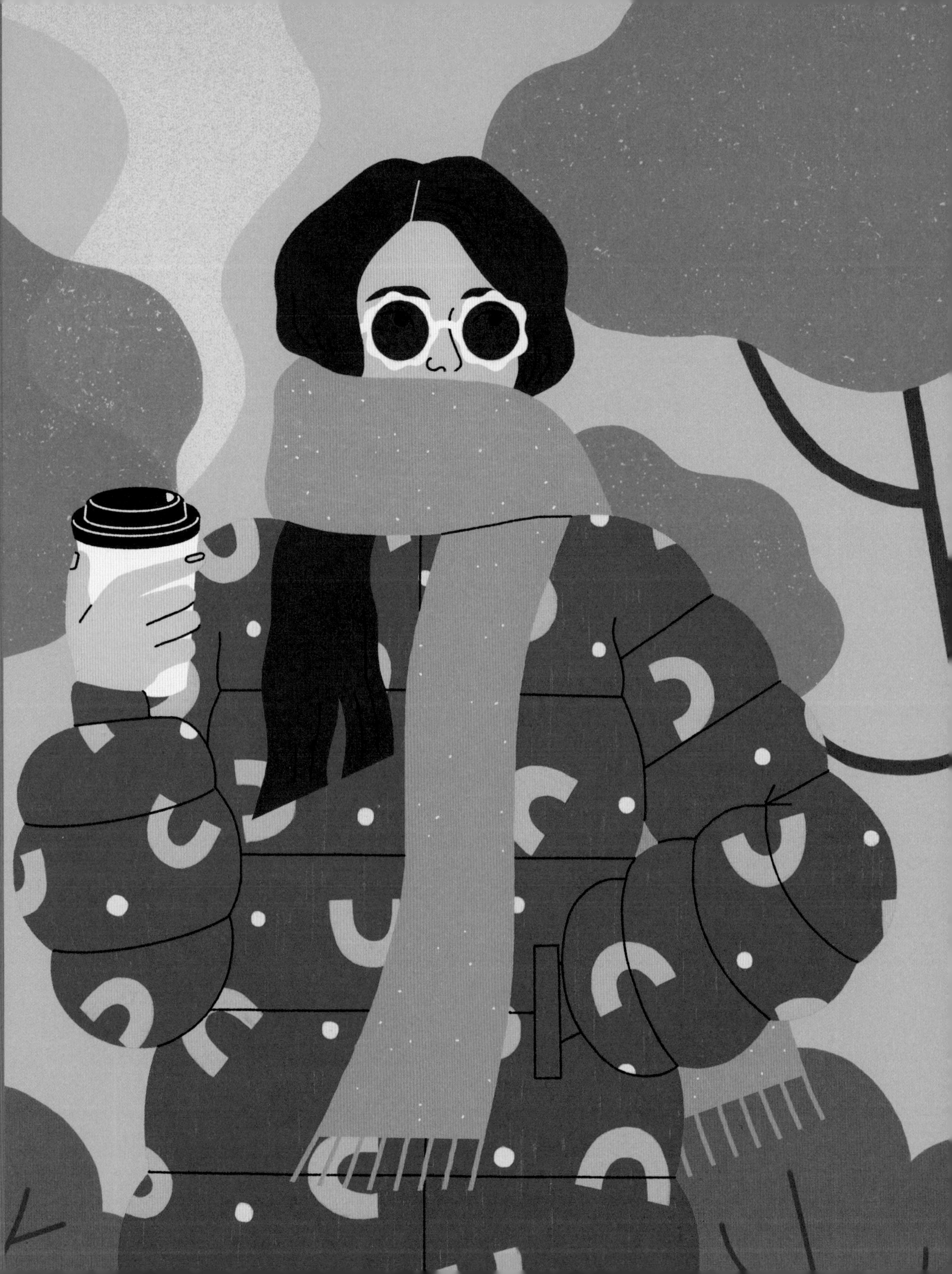

Emotional Regulation

ADHD can be confusing. At times we're able to focus deeply, but then we can swing to being scattered or disruptive. Sometimes we're empathetic, sensitive listeners, and other times we overshare or have an angry outburst. Understanding how our executive functioning and productivity are impacted by emotional dysregulation is crucial. Learning how to become aware of our thought patterns plays a huge role in finding more balance, becoming aware of our emotional habits and starting to rewire those neural pathways.

Imagine a day like Kate's . . .

I wake up, already exhausted because I had insomnia last night. I was up worrying because I sent my friend a long, honest message the other day, and they have read it but still not responded. My thoughts start to spiral into RSD (rejection sensitive dysphoria—see page 63), so to distract myself, I grab my phone from my bedside table and start checking my notifications. I see a calendar reminder: take gym clothes to work. I know I should get up and pack my gym clothes before I forget, but I'm too exhausted to get out of bed. I can't shake the feeling that I've weirded out my friend, and I'm worried that I overshared. Finally, my "get the f**k up" alarm goes off, and I realize I've been ruminating for 20 minutes, and now I'm late. Really late.

As I rush to brew my morning coffee, I notice that my favorite travel mug is missing, and I spend precious time searching for it because there's no way I can face today with the ugly mug. Finally, I find it under the pile of dirty dishes. I'm now running so late that I don't have time to eat or pack lunch, but there's no way I can leave without makeup, so I dash to the bathroom anyway, texting my work bestie that I'll be late. As I do, I realize I forgot to charge my phone last night because I couldn't find my charger, and it's only got 10 percent battery. I spend an extra five minutes searching high and low before deciding to ask someone at work for a charger.

I arrive at work late, in the middle of a team meeting. I feel like everyone is thinking what a hot mess I am. Focusing during the meeting is hard because I'm stressed and hungry. When my boss asks me a question, I have a total mental blank on the answer, even though I know I know it. Arrrgh! After the meeting, I make sure I find a phone charger, and then sit down to work. I'm not in the headspace at all, and as I open my laptop, I remember that binaural beats can help concentration for ADHDers. Instantly, I've got more energy as I start hunting for the perfect playlist. I end up on a hyperfocus deep-dive researching the science of binaural beats and brain waves. Whoops, maybe I shouldn't have spent that long . . .

I get to lunchtime starving because I'd been so stressed about starting work late and charging my phone, I'd forgotten to eat. During the afternoon, I need to do research for an upcoming presentation, but I find myself reading and rereading paragraphs over and over, like the words aren't going in.

After what feels like the longest work day ever, it's almost time to leave. My phone pings with a notification. I realize with a sinking feeling that I'm meant to meet my brother at the river for a jog in 15 minutes, but I forgot my gym clothes . . . sh*t.

Phew, what a day. Sound familiar? Kate could be any one of us on any given day . . .

Executive dysfunction

You may identify with some moments in Kate's story (previous page), or maybe all of them. Thankfully most days aren't as bad as that one, but the ones where everything goes wrong can make us feel like failures. ADHD often involves issues with executive functioning–the mental processes that help us plan, prioritize, organize, pay attention and complete tasks effectively. **Problems in this area are called "executive dysfuction."**

We know we want to live with more ease and be organized, but we seem to experience so much executive dysfunction, it's hard to know where to start.

You've probably been told to set timers and create routines, but I'm guessing your efforts, like mine, are short-lived. Things quickly return to the way they were, triggering a downward spiral into self-doubt and shame. The secret to creating change that lasts is to uncover the **root cause** behind most of our executive dysfunctions and work on addressing that.

"Emotional dysregulation" describes a state where we have trouble managing our emotions (more on pages 47–49). Research over the past two decades suggests a clear relationship between executive dysfunction and emotional dysregulation. This means that emotional dysregulation affects executive dysfunction, and visa versa.

Emotional dysregulation	Executive dysfunction

Knowing this is huge, because it explains why ADHDers experience chronic executive dysfunction. In the story on the previous page, it's easy to view Kate as simply forgetful, disorganized and chaotic. But the executive dysfunction started before she even got out of bed. It was triggered when Kate started RSDing about the text message she'd sent to a friend. Ruminating on that thought set off a chain reaction that affected her whole day.

This is why emotional regulation is a crucial part of an ADHD book about productivity and focus. **Becoming more self-aware of our emotional dysregulation while it's happening is powerful**, because it allows us to build strong neural pathways that obliterate our old ones. This process isn't easy. Believe me, I know how impossible it feels to try and stop a spiral when it starts. But the tools and strategies I suggest in this chapter (ones I've tried and tested myself and with others) give us another option–a way to exit the dysregulation spirals. We won't be able to do it every time–but the good news is that practice reinforces neural pathways. And ADHD gives us lots of opportunities to practice!

There's no quick fix; it's a journey that involves challenging existing beliefs, developing new emotional habits and being patient with ourselves. So, are you willing to trust the process? What have you got to lose?

An emotional roller coaster

Living with ADHD can feel like a roller coaster ride, changing minute by minute. Research indicates a clear link between how ADHDers feel emotions (more intensely and impulsively) and our nervous system's response. People will often ask: "What makes ADHDers more emotional? Aren't **all** humans emotional beings?" It's a good question, but because each person's emotional experience is subjective, it's hard to know what's considered "nomal"—so it's best to focus on what's normal for you.

My whole life, I thought everyone cycled through 14 distinct emotional states in an hour, but my neurotypical husband tells me he doesn't know what that feels like. Does my husband have feelings? Of course. But are they as frequent, intense and all-consuming as mine? No. It's the intensity and seeming brevity of the feelings that can be so hard to fathom for the average neurotypical. I'm ecstatic one minute, and "life is over" the next . . . all because someone is taking too long to reply to an email. My emotional sensitivity can be a strength though. It makes me empathetic and gives me the ability (and desire) to see others' perspectives and hold paradoxical ideas simultaneously.

When we are regulated in our nervous system, we exhibit our ADHD strengths, but when we are dysregulated, we display a completely different set of symptoms. Here are some examples of the difference between regulated and dysregulated traits:

Regulated ADHD	Dysregulated ADHD
Divergent, outside-the-box thinking	Analysis paralysis + decision fatigue
A strong desire for autonomy	May have trouble working in teams
Irrepressible curiosity for new things	Overcommited + burnt out
Empathetic + sensitive listener	Overwhelmed by people + uncontactable
Strong sense of social justice	Fanatical, intense + overzealous
Big picture thinker + visionary	Trouble organizing + executing ideas
Warmth + charisma in relationships	Rejection sensitivity + oversharing
Spontaneous + adventurous	Reckless + impulsive
Deeply focused + highly productive	Procrastination + inattentiveness
Direct + honest	Insensitive + unkind
Innovative + creative	Avoiding rules or instructions

Your thoughts

Think of a time you overshared, procrastinated or experienced analysis paralysis or rejection sensitive dysphoria (RSD). Is it possible you were dysregulated by emotional or physical triggers in the lead-up? Can you trace it back and see the pattern?

We tend to go through patterns with dysregulation, depending on our environment and life season. Look at the list of **dysregulated** ADHD symptoms on the previous page. Which ones have you been feeling lately?

On a scale of 1–10 (10 being the most) how well do you feel you understand your triggers and are able to notice when you're getting dysregulated?

| 1 | 2 | 3 | 4 | 5 | 6 | 7 | 8 | 9 | 10 |

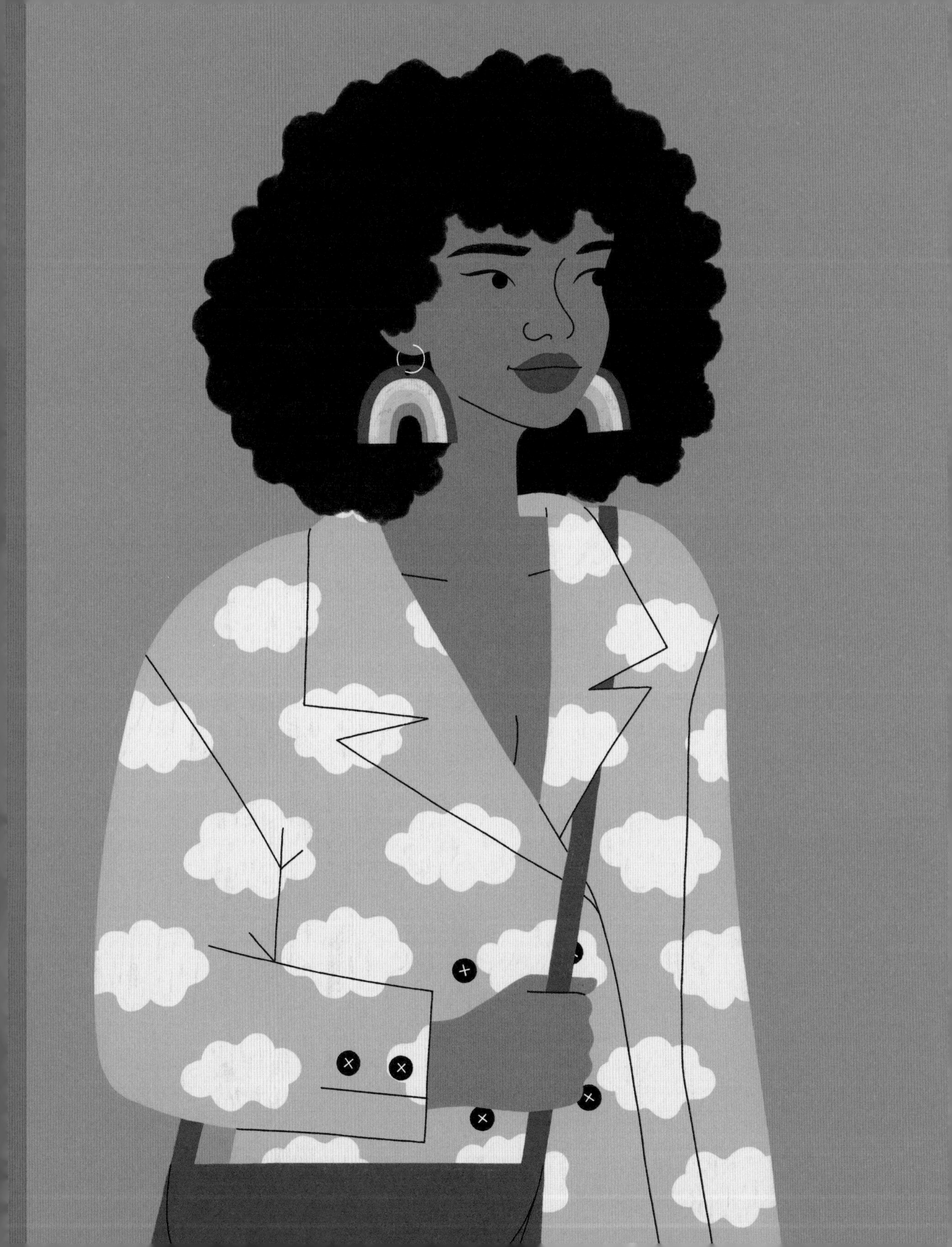

Emotional regulation

Emotional regulation is a key part of ADHD. Studies have found that emotional dysregulation in ADHD is a "major contributor to impairment," and suggest that neurodivergents struggle with regulation more frequently than neurotypicals.

Emotional regulation describes the ability to be **aware** of emotional states and effectively **manage** thoughts and reactions to events. People who are skilled in emotional regulation can respond adaptively to stress, challenges and a variety of social interactions. **Emotional reactions tend to happen instantly for ADHDers**, but when we look at the four steps of emotion below, we can see how emotional regulation plays out in slow motion.

The four stages of emotional regulation (or dysregulation)

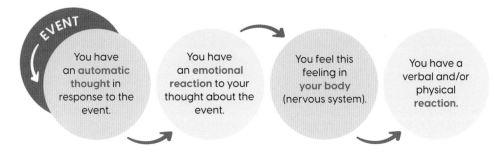

EVENT

You have an **automatic thought** in response to the event.

You have an **emotional reaction** to your thought about the event.

You feel this feeling in **your body** (nervous system).

You have a verbal and/or physical **reaction**.

An example of emotions in slow motion

Applying the model above, let's explore how emotional regulation affects our actions. **Imagine a scenario where a family member pops in to visit unexpectedly and you don't have any food in the house. Let's break down the four stages of emotional dysregulation . . .**

> **1. What is your immediate,** automatic thought?
> I was too disorganized to go shopping this week and now I look stupid.
>
> **2. How do you** feel emotionally **about that thought?**
> I'm a complete failure. I can't "adult" properly and it's because of ADHD.
>
> **3. How do you now feel in your** body?
> Stressed, anxious, jittery, nauseous.
>
> **4. What is your** reaction **as a result?**
> Apologizing so many times it's awkward, getting flustered and anxious.

Interesting, right? We'll revisit these questions again in a few pages.

The dysregulation cycle

We go through these four basic emotional stages thousands of times a day with each micro decision we make. For ADHDers who experience emotions intensely (and without much relief), it's exhausting. Our brains shoot rapid-fire thoughts, and they pile up so fast, they don't allow us processing time. We know emotional regulation would help, but we're inundated. We don't know what to change or how to slow down our thought processes. In this section, I'm going to teach you some thought exercises to give yourself more time and space.

Dysregulation breeds dysregulation—it's a cycle. If we're already dysregulated when we reach Step 1 (see previous page—our thought about an event), we're more likely to think thoughts that activate our stress response (the sympathetic nervous system—more on page 51). This can cause us to make impulsive choices that aren't in our best interests.

Here are some examples . . .

- *We emerge from our room after hyperfocusing for six hours straight. Minutes before we were 100 percent oblivious to our hunger, but now we're starving. Because we're already dysregulated and our emotions are intense, we'll struggle to have a rational thought when we get to Step 2. We'll open the fridge and think: "Argh, there's nothing to eat," and "Making food takes too long." We're no longer hungry, but "hangry," which will feel stressful in our body, so we'll grab a big bag of chips (which also satisfies our sensory needs) instead of making a healthier snack.*

- *Now our appetite is satisfied, but we're likely to get quickly dysregulated again since we haven't eaten a proper meal (and forgot to drink water too). We're getting ready for bed, but as we go to close our laptop, we see a new show on Netflix. We assure ourselves we'll just take a quick look, and then end up bingewatching. Finally, at 3 a.m., our head hits the pillow. We're too tired to brush our teeth or remove our makeup, and forget to set an alarm. We wake up late and overtired, meaning we start our day dysregulated . . . and the cycle continues.*

Your thoughts

Describe a situation where you regularly encounter executive dysfunction. Can you identify whether your executive dysfunction is linked to emotional dysregulation?

Why we get dysregulated

ADHDers become emotionally dysregulated when something (or an accumulation of subtle things) triggers us. Suddenly, we're unable to control our emotions, repress angry outbursts or think logically. It's very stressful, causing turmoil for ADHDers and those around us.

Because neurodivergents are more sensitive (compared to neurotypicals), we can reach sensory overload and become dysregulated more quickly and more often. Loud noises, bright lights, physical sensations (like being too cold, hungry or overstimulated) and emotional triggers like rejection, boredom or conflict can push us into overwhelm.

Intense emotions and sensory overload are painful, and when we become "flooded," we no longer have the tools to cope or emotionally regulate. In these moments, our nervous system is in fight-or-flight . . . we might explode angrily in front of everyone, or implode—which could look like a shutdown or panic attack.

But, from what I've observed, ADHDers may consistently exist in a chronic state of fight-or-flight—appearing composed on the surface but churning emotionally underneath. In this more hidden state of dysregulation, we can become stuck in an unconscious cycle of maladaptive behavior and self-sabotage. What do I mean by maladaptive behavior?

Maladaptive behaviors	make things *easier* in the short term and **harder** in the long term.
We choose maladaptive (unhealthy) behaviors when we're emotionally <u>dysregulated</u>.	

Adaptive behaviors	make things *easier* in the short term and **easier** in the long term.
We choose adaptive (healthy) behaviors when we're emotionally <u>regulated</u>.	

Emotional dysregulation is a repeated unconscious pattern

Emotional regulation strategies are largely learned in childhood by watching the behavioral patterns of our parents, caregivers and other people close to us. Over time, these learned emotional patterns become part of our subconscious reactions—an autopilot setting influencing how we navigate emotions throughout our lives.

Adaptive strategies may be less intuitive for ADHDers because they require the ability to look ahead into the distant future and assess whether a response will make life easier or harder in the long term. Because ADHDers struggle with time blindness and impulsivity, we don't tend to pause and predict negative future outcomes before responding to a situation. We are also prone to choosing maladaptive strategies when we're feeling unsafe (emotionally, socially or physically) and our brain's warning system is on high alert. Let's find out more about the anatomy of the brain's warning system.

Understanding how emotional dysregulation affects our executive functioning and productivity is <u>transformative.</u>

The brain's warning system

The amygdala

Imagine you're faced with a sudden threat like an oncoming car. Your eyes or ears (or both) quickly relay this info to a tiny brain region called the amygdala, which is like our ever-vigilant bodyguard. The amygdala checks out the scene and, if it senses danger, sends out a distress signal to the hypothalamus. The amygdala doesn't alert us just to physical dangers but psychological, emotional and social ones too.

The hypothalamus

The hypothalamus is the brain's command center. It orchestrates communication with the rest of the body through the autonomic nervous system, responsible for handling automatic bodily functions such as respiration, blood pressure regulation, heart rate modulation and the dilation or constriction of blood vessels and lung bronchioles.

The sympathetic nervous system

The autonomic nervous system is split into two branches—the sympathetic and the parasympathetic systems. When the amygdala triggers the alarm, the sympathetic nervous system (fight, flight, or freeze mode) kicks in. It directs your adrenal glands to release epinephrine (adrenaline) and cortisol into your bloodstream. Your heart races, blood flows to vital organs, pulse spikes, blood pressure rises, and you breathe like a sprinter. The body shifts its energy resources towards fighting off a life threat or fleeing from an enemy. Plus, epinephrine directs your body to release stored sugar and fats into your bloodstream for that extra energy boost. This happens in seconds, often before your rational brain catches on, allowing you to instinctively dodge danger, like an oncoming car.

The parasympathetic nervous system

You can't stay in that stress state forever, and once the threat has passed, it's the job of your parasympathetic nervous system to put the brakes on and slow down your heart and breathing rate, and return your body back to a state of rest and recovery. The exercises in the chapter Hello, Nervous System will help you do this.

ADHDers can get stuck in a chronic state of stress

In our modern world, our amygdala might consider many things a "threat" to us—like that email from your boss or a social media post that gives you RSD. Your nervous system is simply trying to warn you of possible dangers; however, because it's so sensitive it becomes hypervigilant. It's clear from both anecdotal evidence and research studies that people with ADHD experience more life stressors. These small stressors accumulate as a chronic stress burden in our nervous system and can cause a range of health issues.

Emotions as habits

One of the biggest "aha" moments for me was learning that almost all my emotional responses are habitual, automatic and unconscious. Emotions are energetic messages shooting through our nervous systems—literally energy in motion (e-motion). We observe stimuli in our environment (internal or external, subtle or obvious), which prompts a cascade of chemical messages in our nervous system, and these are our feelings.

Neural highways

Neural pathways are circuits formed by neurons in the brain to transmit and process information. When we repeatedly think or do something, these pathways become "highways," making the process faster and more automatic. Each day provides an array of experiences—things we've done and seen a thousand times before plus unpredictable, new stimuli. Because our most basic needs are safety and security, our brain is searching for predictability first. The brain's goal is efficiency and, ultimately, survival. By forming associations, anticipating emotional responses and pre-selecting familiar thoughts, our brain constructs mental shortcuts for decision-making. This saves maximum mental energy for dealing with new things and unfamiliar problems.

Automatic, habitual emotions can add fuel to the fire

While anticipating emotions and needs is more efficient for brain/body functioning, it can steer us towards unhealthy, automatic emotional habits. **For ADHDers, this can mean we can make lightning-fast assumptions, going from regulated to dysregulated in seconds.**

Here's an example with RSD (rejection sensitive dysphoria):

The trigger

You invited your friend out for a coffee, but they haven't responded to your text.

Your habitual emotional response

You're sensitive to rejection. Without your conscious awareness, your nervous system triggers the sympathetic response (fight, flight, freeze). Your brain responds to the alarm bells by efficiently giving you an automatically selected "rejection" thought: "I'm being ghosted because I'm too much." This may be negative, but it's a well-worn highway, and the brain likes predicability. If you don't challenge that thought and look for other possible explanations, you'll likely lean hard into RSD and become dysregulated. You'll stop thinking logically, overreact and send a text that could start a conflict.

Read more about RSD on page 63.

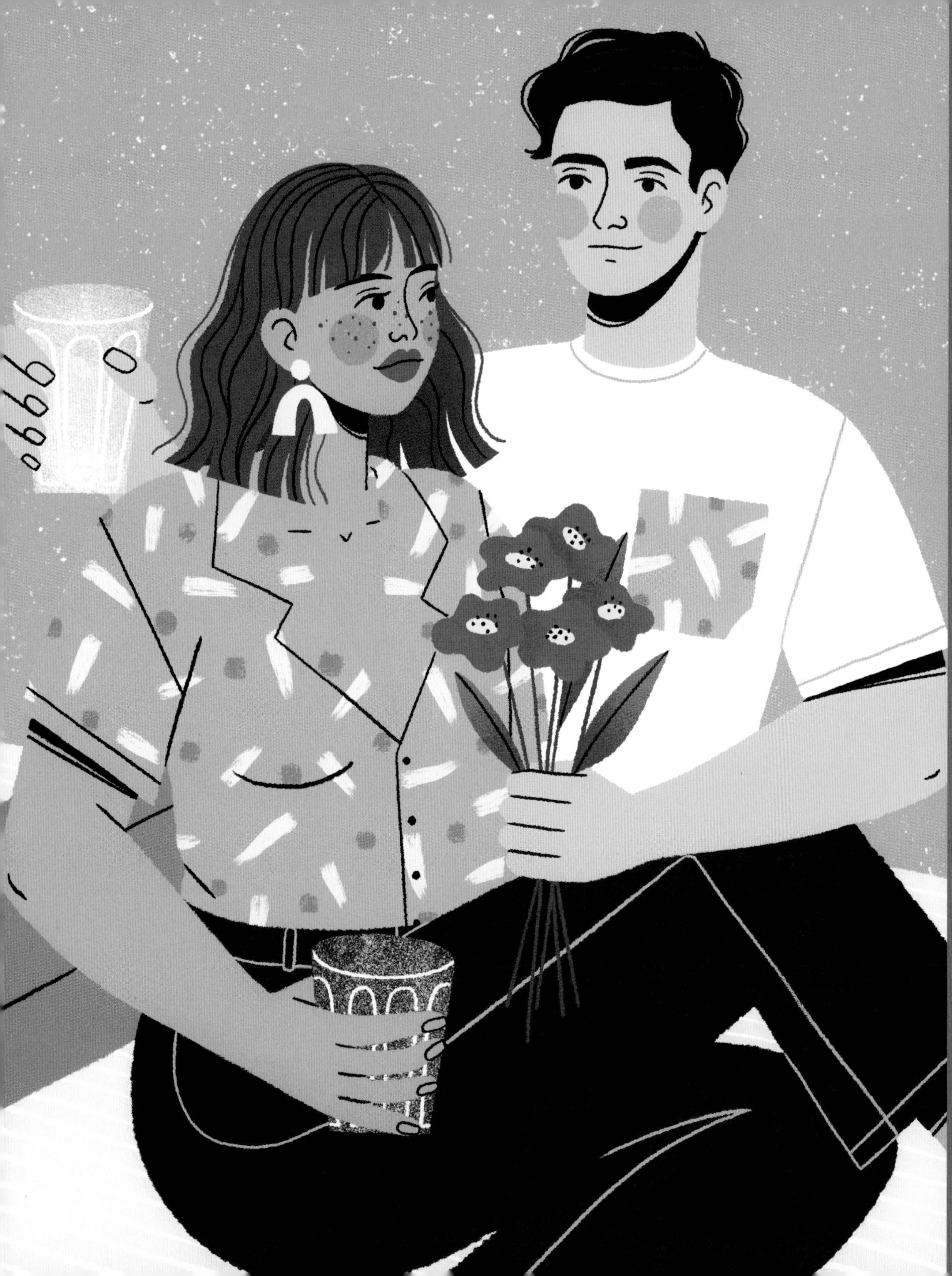

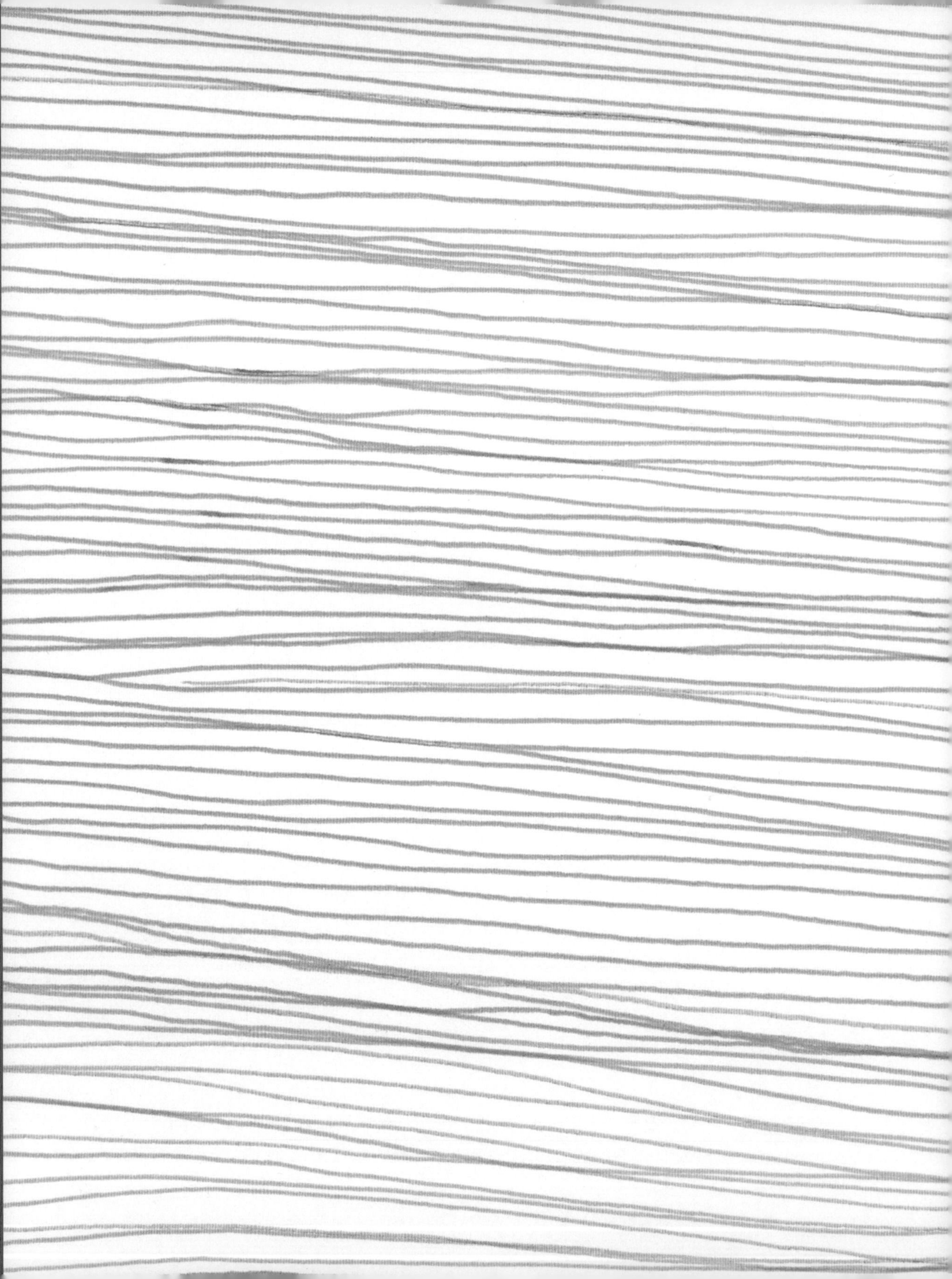

Habit highways

If we want to **stop** jumping automatically to RSD (or other unhelpful emotional behaviors), we need to understand the relationship between habits and neural highways—which I like to call "habit highways." Behaviors and habits are formed by repeated neural activity—when "neurons that fire together, wire together." It's a complex process, but here's how I like to visualize it:

Learning new habits can be a bumpy ride because we are literally doing heavy-duty construction work on our brain. It's messy at first.

All habits are neural pathways that have been traveled so many times, they become smooth like highways. That's why they're more automatic.

When we want to change a habit, we need to stop using the highway, and start bushwhacking through the forest to create a new habit—a new neural pathway.

Then we have to repeatedly travel down that rough path until it becomes smooth like a highway. The old habit highway becomes overgrown and harder to access.

This is why starting a new habit is so painful (ouch, a spiky bush!) and why early repetition is so important, to make the pathway more clear.

Let's explore what happens when automatic thoughts become brain algorithms . . .

At its core, ADHD is really about <u>intensity</u> . . .

Intensity of excitement, intensity of rejection sensitivity. Intensity of focus. Intensity of executive dysfunction.

Our brain's algorithm

We've learned that our brain is pretty resourceful—constantly making our regular behaviors and thought patterns automatic. This saves time and energy, freeing up bandwidth for learning, problem solving and creativity. **Imagine your brain is like Google,** running thousands of searches every day in response to stimuli and events that are happening to you. Your waiter brings you the wrong dish, or your kid starts yelling at you, and bam—your brain is rapidly filtering through thoughts and providing you with what it *thinks* you need—all in the blink of an eye. It's one hell of an unconscious algorithm.

Just as you type keywords into Google to find relevant information, your brain filters through a vast amount of data to focus on what's important to you, and eliminate what's not. This filter, called the reticular activating system, helps you prioritize things that align with your interests and beliefs, known as "confirmation bias."

Studies show our brain <u>automatically</u> assesses whether a situation is:	• new or familiar • relevant or irrelevant to our goals and focus • controllable or beyond control • consistent with our values or not

Google and your brain share the same goal, because they're feedback driven. Neural pathways (algorithms) are created through repetition and feedback. They want to give you quick results that you have high affinity with, which will make you "click." **Just like Google has an algorithm based on your previous search history, our brains bring up a search list of thoughts based on thoughts we've had before.**

The problem with choosing the "clickbait thoughts"

When you do an internet search, sometimes you'll choose the top result, and other times you'll scroll down the search results looking for something else. When your brain responds to a situation, the top thought your brain offers you might be:

factual**analytical****unverifiable****emotionally charged****unreliable**

I've learned my top thought is often emotionally charged or unverifiable (just like real-life clickbait), and I should always keep "scrolling down my search results" to find more reliable thoughts. **What that looks like is actively asking my brain to generate other possible thoughts about that situation and analyzing those.** If I take the first, highly emotional response that comes into my head, I might overlook alternative thoughts and emotions related to the situation that could potentially serve me better.

"Clickbait" is misleading or sensational online content designed to attract clicks.

Clickbait thoughts

As ADHDers, it is sooo tempting to rush into emotions, and pounce on the first clickbait thought our mind generates. The first step in learning to regulate our emotions is building self-awareness.

Let's practice identifying clickbait thoughts (the spicy, often RSD-fueled ones at the top of our brain's search results) and **actively ask our brain to produce more options for us to consider.** Here's a scenario as an example:

Scenario

Thought

🔍 **Your new friend cancels plans at the last minute.**

✳ They don't like me. They're definitely ghosting me.

RSD clickbait alert!

Avoid the clickbait. **Ask your brain to come up with other thoughts.**

🔍 **Your new friend cancels plans at the last minute.**

✳ They don't like me. They're definitely ghosting me.

Something more exciting came up. I'm not fun.

Maybe they're sick.

Maybe they're really stressed and just need some alone time.

Maybe their family needed help.

Maybe they don't want to have to fake it when they're upset.

EXAMPLE 1

Here's another one:

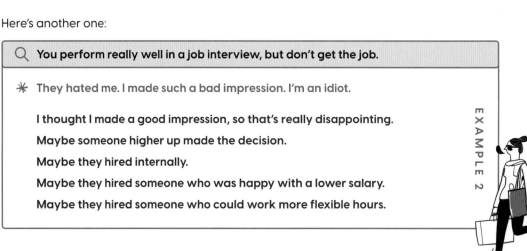

🔍 **You perform really well in a job interview, but don't get the job.**

✳ They hated me. I made such a bad impression. I'm an idiot.

I thought I made a good impression, so that's really disappointing.

Maybe someone higher up made the decision.

Maybe they hired internally.

Maybe they hired someone who was happy with a lower salary.

Maybe they hired someone who could work more flexible hours.

EXAMPLE 2

Okay, now it's your turn to try with your own scenarios:

🔍

✳

🔍

✳

🔍

✳

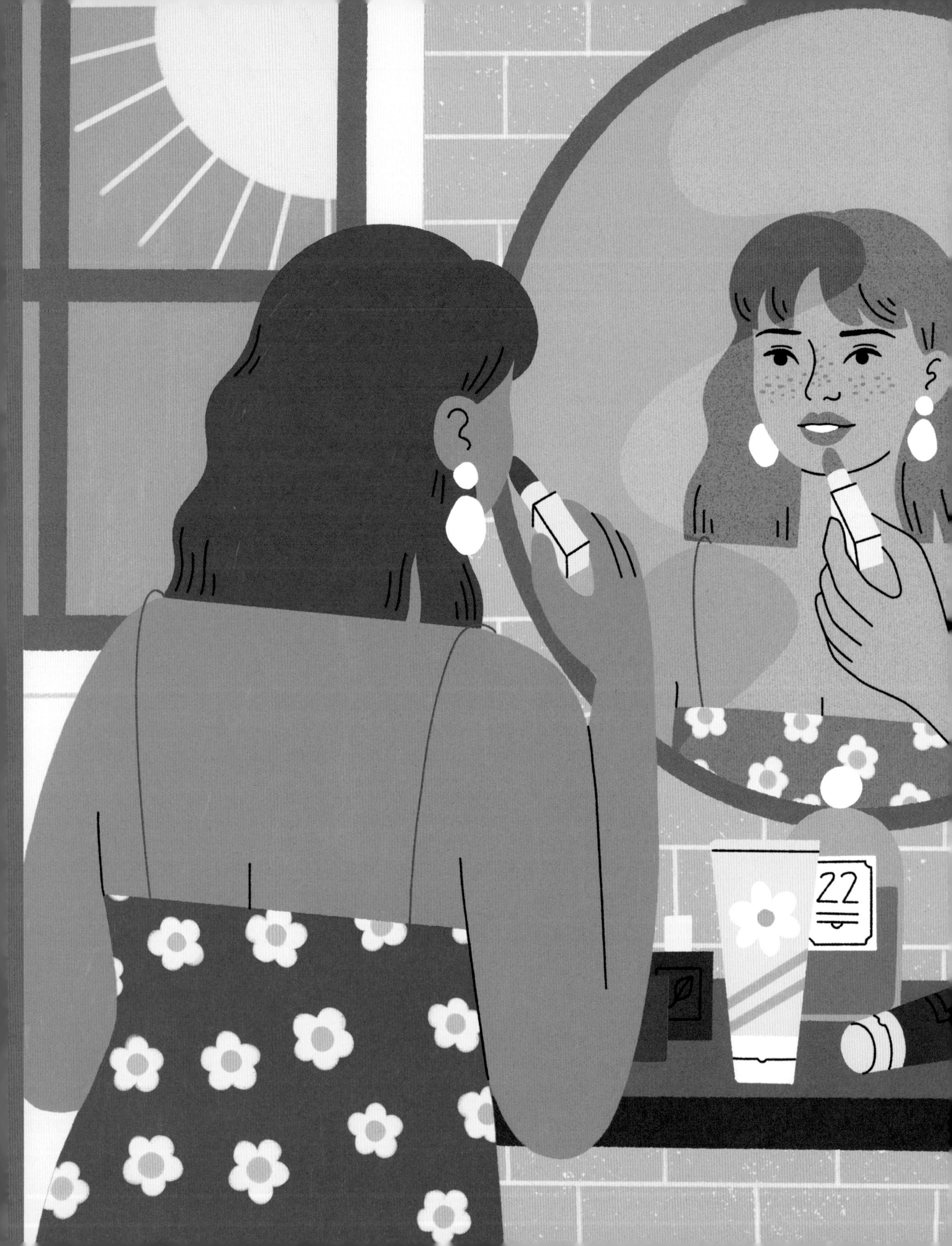
22

We see
things not as
they are, but
as <u>we</u> are.

Anaïs Nin

Assuming the worst

ADHDers are prone to taking the first, most negative interpretation of a situation and running with it. Often our partner, friends or colleagues will say things to us like:

- Don't put words in my mouth
- That's not what I meant
- Where on earth did you get that idea from?

So <u>why</u> have our brains learned to choose the most negative option first and cling to that? Any thought we repeat over and over becomes a neural pathway. Improving our emotional regulation skills means understanding not just **what** we think, but **where** these negative thought patterns originated.

Where do our negative assumptions come from?

Low self-esteem

Our low self-esteem can be a result of childhood adversity and feeling like a failure because we don't measure up to neurotypical norms. (More on page 32.)

Overactive amygdala

Negative experiences, bullying and critical comments from parents, peers, caregivers and teachers are triggers that are imprinted in our nervous system. When something happens in the present, the amygdala (our feisty little bodyguard) fires up because it notices a threat, whether this is factual or imagined. Our amygdala is overly protective because we've been hurt before. Internal Family Systems therapy helps you approach that protective part with appreciation, and work with it to release its pain and shame. Often this part just needs to understand you're no longer a child and can look after yourself. Then the protective part feels safe to step back and let you work things out without being crippled by fear.

Combine this with impulsivity and you get a heady cocktail!

All-or-nothing thinking

ADHDers are prone to rigid extremes in thinking. It's often described as "going from 0 to 100," or "all-or-nothing thinking." It stems from a tendency towards emotional and behavioral perfectionism, where we believe things need to feel perfect and play out exactly as we imagined in order to be right. According to perfectionism expert Katherine Morgan Schafler, if a goal isn't reached in the perfect manner imagined, we may consider the entire project a failure. This applies to experiences, conversations and relationships too.

Rejection sensitive dysphoria (RSD)

"Rejection sensitive dysphoria" (or RSD) is a term used in the neurodivergent community to describe the intense fear of rejection or criticism in social settings, family relationships, workplaces and beyond. RSD is like having an extra-sensitive emotional antenna that's always on the lookout for signs of rejection or criticism. Even a harmless comment can feel like a major hit, which we feel physically and often for many days. Many people say it's the most debilitating symptom of their ADHD.

RSD (or "RSDing") can look like:

- Reacting with anger or intense emotion to criticism or rejection
- Avoiding opportunities because we don't want to fail
- Rehearsing conversations in our head over and over
- Being overly self-criticial
- Bursting into tears at the smallest offense
- Apologizing too much and people-pleasing
- Overthinking and exessive rumination after conversations or parties

RSD and clickbait thoughts

We succumb to the clickbait version of a thought all the time when it comes to rejection. My theory is that because ADHDers are more emotional, sensitive and intense than neurotypical types, our reticular activating systems are extremely attuned to rejection. Neurodivergents tend to have a history being bullied, excluded in social groups, or ghosted. Because of this painful experience, our amygdala (the fight, flight, or freeze response) wants to protect us, and goes into overdrive as soon as our reticular activating system picks up data that might signal we're about to experience rejection.

These negative thoughts from the amygdala are clickbait thoughts (which usually don't serve us). I'm going to show you how to avoid the clickbait thoughts in the next exercise.

Avoiding the clickbait

Your thoughts = emotions = actions. **If you can resist the worst-case scenario (the clickbait) and input a different thought, you can break the cycle of dysregulation.** I'm going to show you how to do this with the job interview example from before.

> $\mathbb{Q}$ **You perform really well in a job interview, but don't get the job.**
>
> RSD clickbait alert! →
>
> ✳ They hated me. I made such a bad impression. I'm an idiot.
>
> I thought I made a good impression, so that's really disappointing.
>
> Maybe someone higher up made the decision.
>
> Maybe they hired internally.
>
> Maybe they hired someone who was happy with a lower salary.
>
> Maybe they hired someone who could work more flexible hours.

First, let's try with the clickbait thought:

1. **What is your thought?** ✳ They hated me, I made a bad impression. I'm an idiot.

2. **How do you feel about that thought?** I hate myself and feel depressed.

3. **How do you now feel in your body?** Heavy, dull, achy, exhausted.

4. **What is your action as a result?** Binge Netflix for days and stop applying for jobs.

Now we'll pick another thought from further down the list:

1. **What is your thought?** Maybe they hired someone who could work flexible hours.

2. **How do you feel about that thought?** Interested, curious, contemplative.

3. **How do you now feel in your body?** Light, energetic.

4. **What is your action as a result?** Wondering if I could be more flexible on hours which might give me an advantage in the next interview? Back to the job search!

It's remarkable how resisting the clickbait thought and actively seeking alternative interpretations changes our feeling about the event, which changes our actions . . . which can change our lives. Now it's your turn to bring it all together with an example from your own life!

🔍

✳

First, let's try with the clickbait thought:

1. What is your thought? ✳

2. How do you feel about that thought?

3. How do you now feel in your body?

4. What is your action as a result?

Now pick another thought from further down your list:

1. What is your thought? ✳

2. How do you feel about that thought?

3. How do you now feel in your body?

4. What is your action as a result?

> **When we unlock 'why' we are, we also unlock 'how' we can be. Understanding yourself is transformative.**
>
> *Georgie*

Georgie's story

I remember hearing it my whole life. When I was a young girl, it was: "Slow down! Can't you sit still? You got into the gifted and talented program. Stop touching everything!" In my teenage and young adult years, it was: "How many days has it been since you showered? You've been doing that for hours, can't you come have dinner with the family? You have so much potential, but you don't focus." As I entered my mid-to-late twenties, they'd say: "Why are you doing it like that? You're funny! I have no idea what you're talking about."

And then one day, someone said it differently: "It's almost like you've got ADHD." I laughed it off, then went and Googled it for four hours straight. In that moment, everything made complete sense. Suddenly I could explain why I was so different—why chores could be so easy sometimes (productive procrastination) and impossible other times (executive dysfunction) . . . why I was sometimes the most adventurous person you've ever met and other times a burnt-out hermit . . . why I could be tenacious and perfectionistic enough to be promoted at work but at the same time give up on a hobby after a week.

I could make friends easily, and my natural empathy and intuition meant connecting with people on the deepest level . . . but I also found it so hard to keep friendships working due to poor memory, time blindness, overcommitting, oversharing and RSD.

Realizing I have ADHD has been transformative. Just nine months into my self-diagnosis journey, my entire outlook on myself has changed. It has allowed me to love myself, to be compassionate, to understand myself and to support myself in healing and growth.

My partner is my best friend; he's known me for many years and has an interesting perspective on my diagnosis journey. "You're more ADHD than you were before," he observed. "Your symptoms are more obvious since you started researching it, but I think that's because you're more comfortable in your own skin now; you hide less. I think you're happier, and that makes me happier."

For all those people out there making yourself seem less or different from the weird person you are when you're at home alone: I see you, I am with you and you make perfect sense to me.

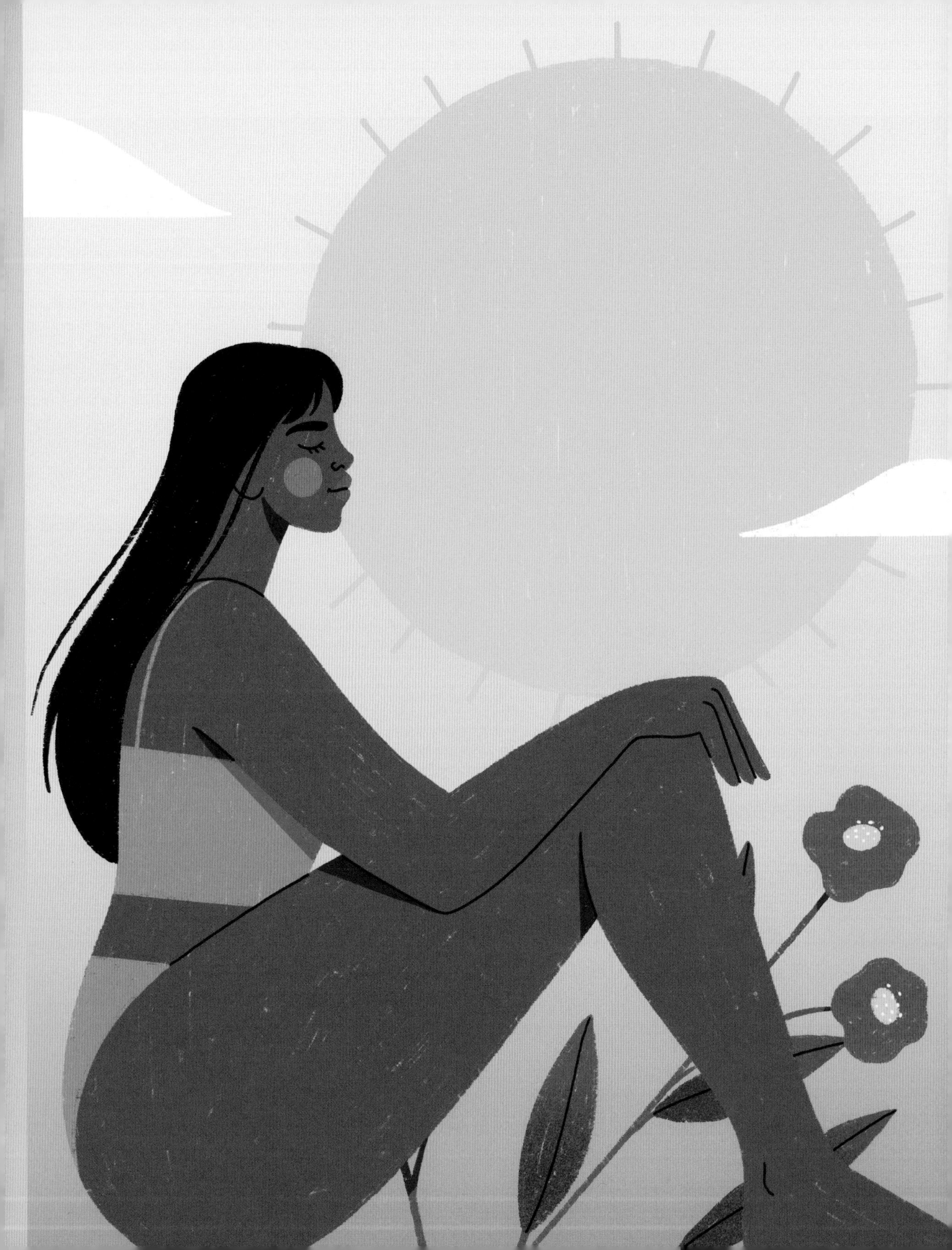

Hello, Nervous System

People with ADHD tend to have sensitive nervous systems. Subtle (or not so subtle) triggers in our environments can quickly dysregulate our nervous system, such as repetitive noises, boredom, crowds, cluttered spaces and other people's emotions. Learning how to move from fight-or-flight back into balance and calm is a game changer. Nervous system nourishment helps us manage stress and brings our executive functions back online.

Nervous system 101

In order to grasp the full picture of ADHD, we need to take a deep dive into the nervous system. Understanding our nervous system and learning to downregulate it (calm it down) is a valuable tool for ADHDers. In simple terms, when our nervous system is frazzled and worn out, ADHD symptoms like forgetfulness, lethargy, demand avoidance, working memory and RSD will be far worse. Our experience with ADHD can fluctuate—being challenging in certain periods and less troublesome in others. (For more, check out page 44.)

What is the nervous system?

The body's nervous system is a complex network made up of the brain, spinal cord and billions of nerves throughout the body. It controls much of what we think and feel, and manages a lot of the bodily functions we don't think about, like heart rate, breathing, digestion and temperature regulation. The nervous system helps all the parts of the body communicate with each other. It's also vigilant, picking up on thousands of subtle cues in our external environment and inside our body, and relaying that information to the brain.

The nervous system comprises two main parts:

The central nervous system	*controls messages between neurons in your brain and spinal cord.*
The peripheral nervous system	*controls messages to and from the rest of your body (including your fight-or-flight responses).*

Bottom-up nervous system messages

When I talk about the nervous system here, I'm talking about that peripheral nervous system, and what's sometimes known as our "bottom-up" messaging pathways: signals coming from the body up to the brain. "Top-down" messages are signals from the brain that travel down into the body. A mind-body approach to ADHD takes into consideration both the top-down **and** the bottom-up messages.

Top-down messages =

Mental processing

↓

Body's sensory receptors

Bottom-up messages =

Mental processing

↑

Body's sensory receptors

A lot of therapies and tools for ADHDers focus on being aware of our top-down messages and changing those in order improve our behavior (e.g., just meditate more, use the Pomodoro method, "eat the frog").

But anyone with ADHD knows it's not as simple as training our brains to "behave better." A mind-body approach to ADHD means listening to our nervous system's bottom-up messages and learning what to do to calm our nervous system when it's dysregulated or distressed.

I've devoted a whole section to the nervous system in this book, because while I've included some top-down, convergent thinking approaches (such as the Clickbait Thoughts exercise–pages 58–59 and 64–65), **it's crucial that you partner with your nervous system as you try these exercises and frameworks**. You may have every intention of being productive, but if your nervous system registers that coffee machine buzzing or the bright lights overhead as irritable, you'll be fighting a losing battle. If you ignore those signals, the messages will pile up, and you'll get progressively more dysregulated, making your ADHD symptoms worse.

ADHD nervous systems have a variety of high-stimulation and low-stimulation needs, and these vary between individuals. For example, one day at work might be easier with people around, and the next it might be too stimulating and you only want music on. Another day you may need total silence–and these fluctuating needs are valid.

Warning: Ignoring your nervous system and forging ahead

A lot of my issues with ADHD come from ignoring my nervous system, forcing myself forward and then spiralling into overwhelm and not knowing how to pull myself out of it.

If you're not sure exactly what a message from your nervous system might feel like, imagine that you **burn your finger**. Bottom-up processing alerts you straightaway. What's your next step? You'll likely say putting your finger straight under running water and keeping it there for at least 10 minutes. But what if you ignored your burn and it got infected? The pain would be throbbing in the background constantly and affect your ability to do tasks or think straight. You'd get stuck in a dysregulated cycle.

People with ADHD tend to have more sensitive nervous systems than neurotypicals, and that means we get "burned" more often. Maybe we learn to tune out our bottom-up messages because there are just too many to process. Or perhaps we didn't have the skills to"treat the burn" so we stopped listening to those pain receptors because . . . what's the point?

When ADHDers ignore the messages that signal we're distressed, overextended, unsafe or exhausted, it's like ignoring a burnt finger. Our first step is to diagnose the problem by learning to listen to our nervous system (e.g., "I'm dysregulated. I need to regulate myself."). The second step is to reach into our toolbox of sensory activities that calm our nervous system when it's stressed. Over time, nervous system regulation can become habitual.

Overstimulation

Neurospicy folks can frequently experience sensory overload (or the feeling of being over-stimulated). ADHD brains are incredibly sensitive to environmental stimuli, often compared to a faucet turned on at full force, inundating them with a deluge of sensory input. **Sensory overload occurs when we reach capacity with the amount of stimuli we can take in.** We get overwhelmed and freeze, like a computer that has too many tabs open.

Overstimulation is caused by:

Too much data

busy places, notifications, conversations, news sites

Too many sensory inputs

bright lights, clutter, crowds, music, loud voices, perfumes

Too much choice

shopping, dating apps, movies and TV, booking websites

When we're overstimulated we may:

- feel irritable, snap at others
- feel on the verge of tears
- have an angry outburst
- feel like we're rushing everywhere
- want to hide
- procrastinate
- stop communicating
- want to block out the world
- overshare
- become more sensitive
- overthink everything
- feel exhausted
- be anxious
- be more forgetful
- be unable to speak coherently

Things that might help:

- go on a screen time fast
- get out into nature
- breathwork exercises
- listen to binaural beats or brown noise
- use sound-isolating head-phones
- use a weighted blanket

Your thoughts

Where are some environments or situations where you regularly find yourself getting <u>overstimulated</u> or reaching <u>sensory overload</u>?

What are telltale signs that you're becoming overstimulated (e.g., headache, verge of tears)?

Which strategies from the previous page might help you in those situations? Do you have any other strategies that work for you that weren't listed?

Understimulation

Understimulation happens when **your brain or body isn't getting enough sensory input to keep it stimulated and regulated**. Research suggests that people with ADHD produce lower levels of dopamine, which can lead to feeling understimulated in situations that other people are typically comfortable in. At times, understimulation can feel physically painful.

Understimulation is caused by:

Boredom

craving intellectual, social, physical or creative stimulation

Simplicity

seeking challenges and avoiding tasks that are too easy

Repetition

finding once-interesting tasks boring once they become routine

---

✳ Author and adventurer Thom Hartmann calls the constant ADHD need for stimulation "the need to feel alive," which is a reframe that I love.

When we're understimulated we may:

- lose motivation and focus
- become hyperactive or reckless
- pick a fight
- become jittery and restless
- become jumpy and anxious
- daydream
- return to addictive behaviors
- binge eat
- get irritable
- overspend
- experience insomnia
- bite nails or pick skin
- procrastinate
- feel flat

Things that might help:

use a stimming toy

learn something new

exercise or dancing

body doubling

explore & act on a whim

listen to podcasts or music

Read more about body doubling on page 111.

Your thoughts

Are there some environments or situations where you regularly find yourself understimulated, restless and bored?

What are telltale signs that you're understimulated (e.g., overspending, picking a fight)?

Which strategies from the previous page might help you in those situations? Do you have any other strategies that work for you that weren't listed?

Interoception means becoming more aware of your bodily sensations. These subtle cues signal that you're becoming dysregulated and remind you to <u>find ways</u> <u>to return</u> to a regulated state.

Interoception

While empirical research on ADHD and interoception is still relatively uncommon, some studies suggest that people with ADHD are less aware of the physical signals and cues in their bodies. **Becoming more aware of your bodily sensations can provide early indicators that you're becoming dysregulated and remind you to find ways to return to a regulated state.**

What's interoception?

"Interoception" is the internal perception and awareness of bodily sensations and physiological states. It's like our body's internal radar, and helps us tune in to all those signals our body sends us—like an increased heartbeat, hunger, thirst, whether we need to go to the bathroom, or whether we're too hot or too cold. This built-in GPS helps us figure out if we're feeling excited, tired, nauseous or anxious. So, whether it's realizing we need a snack or recognizing those butterflies in our stomach before a big presentation, interoception keeps us in sync with what's happening inside and gives us data we can use to modify our behavior.

Interoception difficulties with ADHD

People with ADHD often find it difficult to pick up on interoceptive signals because of the intensity of our emotional and focused states. If we're RSDing, worrying or hyperfocusing, we can forget to eat or binge mindlessly, hold on too long for the bathroom, shiver in cold or forget to drink water. Interoception difficulties in ADHD could also influence emotional awareness, making it challenging to understand what's causing sudden mood swings. Guided meditation, breathwork, somatic dance, yoga and cold plunges can help us connect with our body and become more sensitive to those subtle signals. Working with an ADHD dietitian can help improve interoceptive awareness too.

Want to practice interoception?

Try the Sensory Cocoon Visualization (on page 85). Or you could try a body scan—a mindfulness practice where you attentively focus on various body parts, usually from toes to head. The aim is to observe sensations, tension or discomfort in each part without judgement.

 If being in your body causes you distress due to previous trauma, please explore this work with a trauma-informed mental health professional.

Reminder: play is rest too.

10 types of rest

Psychologist and researcher Nicola Jane Hobbs is one of the leading experts on rest and the nervous system and writes: "Rest is more than napping. Rest is anything that makes our nervous systems feel safe enough for our stress responses to switch off so our minds and bodies can recover and restore." Nicola created a guide to the 10 types of rest, which she's generously allowed me to adapt here.

Physical rest
naps, nutrition, breathwork, gentle yoga, walking

Emotional rest
journaling, "saying no," taking a break from the news

Cognitive rest
non-thinking activities like cooking, bingeing a trashy TV show

Sensory rest
soothing scents, weighted blankets, loose clothing, baths

Psychosocial rest
solitude, friendship, anti-discrimination work, community

Spiritual rest
protecting your energy flow, poetry, meditation

Altruistic rest
volunteering, acts of kindness, donating resources or funds

Ecological rest
time in nature, ocean sounds, nurturing house plants, playing with pets

Playful rest
sports, adventuring, watching comedy, board games, camping

Creative rest
painting, singing and making music, dancing, writing

Triggers & glimmers

Triggers

When the brain is triggered, it associates a painful past experience with something that's happening now. This stimulates our fight-or-flight response, leaving us anxious, emotionally dysregulated and on high alert. As triggers hit, our nervous system goes into action mode, tweaking our heart rate, breathing, muscles and even hormones. Being hypersensitive to triggers can feel like living life with the volume turned way up, and it's exhausting. "Trauma" is a sensitive word, and it's personal for each person. It can be linked to childhood, or negative past experiences like missing a flight, being criticized by your boss or an argument with a friend.

Remember the brain's reticular activating system? It detects and filters triggers (sensory stimuli) to keep us safe. For example, walking out of a bar alone at night may trigger you to stand with other people as you wait for your ride. But traumas like being bullied as a child or harshly criticized by your parents can trigger you too. Researchers have estimated that **ADHD children receive 20,000 more negative messages** than their peers without ADHD, so we will likely get triggered more often, leading to emotional dysregulation and executive functioning breakdown. Inner child work can really help you become aware of your triggers and learn to be less reactive. (I have tried Internal Family Systems therapy and narrative therapy and found both very beneficial.)

Glimmers

Glimmers are the opposite of triggers. They're an external or internal cue that give you a sense of joy or safety. You know those moments where your senses are truly delighted by something? Glimmers can be items, places, foods, sensory inputs, certain people, experiences or even memories that instantly make you feel happy, safe or comforted. It could be a gentle headbutt from a loving pet, warmth from a wood fire, a freshly brewed coffee, a friend's contagious laugh, hearing the rain on the roof, seeing a rainbow, strumming your guitar or getting all the green traffic lights. Glimmers don't have to be glamorous or expensive, and they don't have to make sense to anyone but **you.**

People with ADHD often have nervous systems that are stuck in fight-or-flight and are unable to flexibly move between states of stress and self-soothing. Making a practice of actively noticing glimmers can help remind our nervous system that we are safe, and calm our bodies and minds. So, take a moment each day to consciously notice your glimmers.

We created a prompt in our Take 10, Every 10 review pages where you can note down your triggers and glimmers (see page 127).

When self-care is stressful

In seasons when we're overworked or burnt out, self-care can seem like just another task on our to-do list. Running on stress or adrenaline means that slowing down might feel uncomfortable; like if you were listening to loud music and someone suddenly switched it off—the silence would be extremely jarring. Our bodies like to experience emotions that are familiar, and slowing down is an unfamiliar state that your body interprets as a threat. Here are some ideas if self-care feels too hard for you right now . . .

Tip #1: Normalize it

To help create familiarity with self-care, normalize it. Notice things you're already doing that are self-care, like showering, eating breakfast, walking the dog, listening to podcasts or brushing your teeth.

Tip #2: Activate nostalgia

Start by picking a self-care activity that has some nostalgia attached. This creates familiarity and safety, which will help you transition more easily.

- ☑ Watch a favorite childhood movie
- ☑ Listen to a music album from your teen years
- ☑ Look through old photo albums
- ☑ Read a book you loved as a child or teen

Tip #3: Start with a minute

Start with just a minute of self-care instead of feeling like you have to fill an hour or two. Our ADHD brains can be drawn into all-or-nothing thinking, where we assume that if we can't set aside an hour to do a self-care activity, it's not worth doing at all. **Remind yourself that every minute counts, like every sip of water hydrates your body.**

Tip #4: Acclimatize gradually and ask for help

Be kind to yourself and go slow. You can build up from a minute here or there and acclimatize to longer self-care sessions. Over time your body and mind will feel more comfortable slowing down. Request help if you need it! You could ask a friend to body double (see page 111) with you and do a self-care activity together.

Breathwork exercises

Intentional breathing (or "breathwork") can calm us down by getting rid of a stress hormone called cortisol. When we're stressed, our breathing tends to become quick and shallow. Our body accumulates cortisol and heightens the stress response. It's a cycle of dysregulation. We can reduce cortisol by breathing it off, using breathwork exercises. With slow, deep exhales, we interrupt that dysregulation cycle and signal to our nervous system that it can relax.

When I discovered breathwork as a way to calm my nervous system, I loved it so much I became a certified breathwork and meditation teacher. Breathwork is free, easy to learn and can discretely be done in one minute—almost anywhere! You can do it in the car, your office, your bathroom (sneak out when you have guests), in nature or in bed before sleep. Even just 60 seconds of conscious breath will rapidly engage your parasympathetic nervous system and decrease cortisol. If you're interested in reading more, I'd recommend *Breath* by James Nestor.

 Try these three simple breathwork techniques to quickly move your nervous system from dysregulation to a regulated state.

Box breathing

Box breathing (or "square breathing") is a stress-reduction and relaxation technique that sends a "safe" signal to the brain. A five-minute box breathing practice can decrease stress, boost your immune system and digestion and enhance sleep.

Close your eyes, get comfy sitting or lying down and breathe in this pattern:

Inhale for 4, hold for 4, exhale for 4, hold for 4.

You can increase the "box" to 5, 6 or 8 equal counts if comfortable.

Mountain breath

This is often called 4-7-8 breath, but I like to pair with a visualization and call it "mountain breath."

Breathe in from your belly for 4 counts, and imagine you're climbing a mountain (or going up a chairlift). **Hold** at the top for 7 counts, and visualize the view. **Release and exhale** slow and controlled for 8 counts (or as long as you can). If 4-7-8 is too challenging, begin with 3-4-6 instead. Repeat for two to three minutes and feel your body relax, and your nervous system downregulate.

Bee Breath

In this breath, you simply take a deep breath in, close your lips and slowly exhale (for five to ten seconds), letting out a long hum—just like a bee. The sound of humming is grounding for the nervous system and stimulates the vagus nerve, moving you into a "rest-and-digest" state (calm state).

Repeat three to five times.

WARNING: These exercises are gentle, but listen to your body and don't hold your breath for longer than is comfortable. Speak to your doctor if you have pre-existing medical conditions.

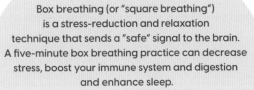

Nourish your nervous system

Guided meditation

Meditation can feel impossible when you have an overactive mind that won't shut off, but the trick with ADHD is to combine meditation with a familiar stimming activity. Try guided visualizations (there are lots of free apps, like Insight Timer), progressive muscle relaxation, walking meditation, dancing meditation (slow swaying movements) or eating meditation (where you're mindful of every sensation and bite).

Sensory cocooning

Sensory cocooning is one of my go-to strategies because it's free, using what you already have at home. Try it when your nervous system is overstimulated or frazzled. You'll need an eye mask, headphones, your phone, an app like Insight Timer or Spotify and a place you won't be disturbed. Try listening to binaural beats, brown noise, Tibetan singing bowls or solfeggio frequencies. Or try the visualization on page 85.

Cuddling animals

If you have pets, you'll know that a cuddle with a dog, cat or other furry friend can be so grounding for the nervous system. Patting a pet releases oxytocin (the feel-good chemical) and lowers cortisol. If you don't have pets, going to a farm, petting zoo or horseback riding so you can spend time outdoors is a really healthy way to de-stress and get some screen-free nature time as well. Your nervous system will thank you for it!

Somatic dance

Finding healthy somatic (body-based) ways to release intense emotions like anger or rage is very important for the ADHD nervous system. Move intuitively to rhythmic music in a safe, private space. You don't have to be a good dancer—try swaying, raising your arms above your head and throwing them down forcefully towards your hips, or stamping with your fists on your thighs. You can also vocalize with low guttural groans.

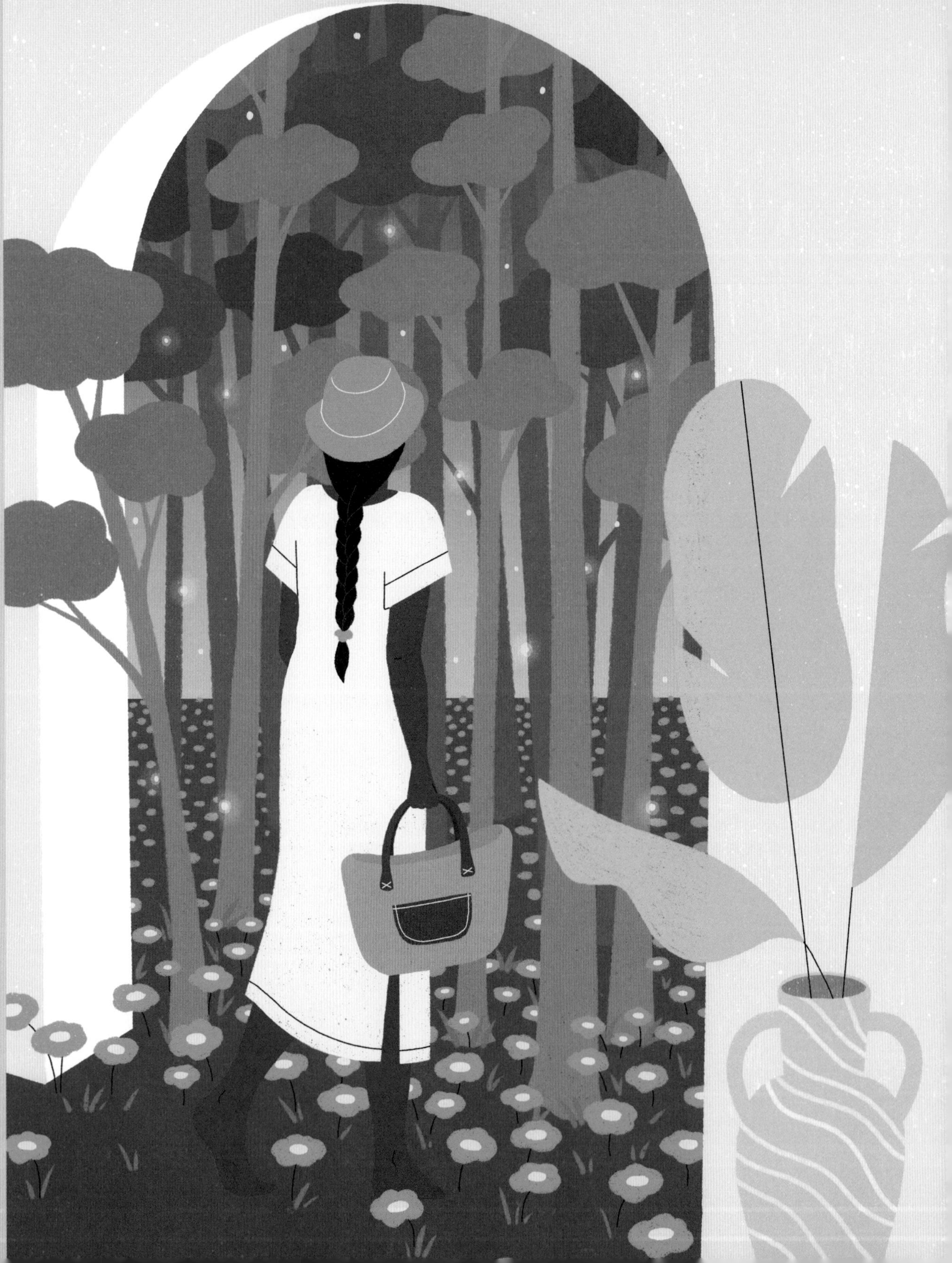

Sensory cocoon visualization

Read the visualization before you begin, or you can ask someone to read it out to you. You can listen to a full version of this visualization at futureadhd.com/deeprest.

Your breath will bring you home to meet yourself, time and time again.

Breathe in deeply through your nose . . . filling up your lungs through the belly right up into your chest. Hold here. You're breathing in this clean air, this permission to exist in the world just as you are. No masks. No expectations. Let go with a deep cleansing sigh.

Imagine that this space is now your deep rest zone. In this space there are no demands on you, and no one needs you. Imagine all the parts of your external world . . . your responsibilities . . . work commitments . . . family relationships . . . outside stresses. See them like white noise or a news station playing on your phone.

Visualize holding your phone in front of you and looking at this white noise playing. And now, visualize pressing the mute button. You're turning down the volume on the outside world, just for a few minutes while we rest in this space . . . this cocoon.

This is your space to nourish your nervous system. It's quiet. You're here in your body. Imagine this sensory cocoon . . . a place you can go to rest. If you could turn off your responsibilities and take a hiatus, where would you go? A retreat in the mountains? A cabin by a stream? A cozy hammock on the beach? Imagine your place now. Take yourself there, and find a comfortable chair or resting place. Wrap your arms around yourself to create this safe cocoon and rock gently.

As you sit or lay there in your sensory cocoon, what do you see in your field of vision? Notice the sounds. The temperature. The smells. Perhaps the softness of a blanket. How does your body feel in this space? Light, sparkly, vivid, soft, pixelated, blurry?

Before you leave this space, let your body know that you've memorized the sights, smells and temperature as a felt sense in your body—in your unconscious mind—and you know how to return to this sensory cocoon again.

Wrap your arms around yourself in a hug, and tell your body that you want to come back again soon . . . that you want to care for it and learn its language. Gently start to bring your awareness away from your internal world now. Feel the solid surface beneath you. Listen to the sounds outside. Wriggle your fingers and toes, blink open your eyes and prepare to return to your day.

ADHDers have interest-based nervous systems. We either struggle to start, or struggle to <u>stop.</u>

Interest-based nervous systems

ADHDers not only struggle to regulate emotions like anger or fear, but also our curiosity. A huge part of our distractibility is caused by our sudden desire to do something on a whim— be it clean out our sock drawer, buy a new set of paints, or research the collective noun of a group of owls (it's a parliament—yes, I know you were wondering!).

Psychiatrist William Dodson theorized the concept of an "interest-based nervous system" to explain how neurodivergent individuals experience the world differently from neurotypicals (who have "importance-based nervous systems," according to Dodson). He suggests ADHDers are typically driven by interest, novelty, competition and urgency. Like Dodson, I believe we are attracted to these things because of inherent and default wiring in our nervous systems. **At the heart of ADHD, I observe four fundamental traits.**

Curiosity

This isn't just passing interest, it's intense and lifelong. We're boredom averse, and curiosity is the antidote to boredom. We don't just love learning, exploring and researching—we live for it! As one ADHDer put it, "I'm thirsty for knowledge and it never feels enough."

Sensitivity

Studies show ADHDers are hyper-responsive to external and internal stimuli, picking up every piece of incoming data and struggling to filter it. The constant barrage can be intense and dysregulating, but also means we can make insightful connections.

Intensity

Call it passion or intensity—this trait is lightning in a bottle. It sees us locked in deep conversation for hours on end, outlasting everyone. It helps us gather speed on projects and hyperfixations, rapidly covering a lot of ground. It can also be exhausting and overwhelming.

Enthusiasm

ADHDers are known for being able to get so excited about certain things, we become emotionally overwhelmed. While this trait can mean others find us "too much," it's a magnetic match for finding our tribe and connecting us with people who are on our wavelength.

Tara's story

ADHD AND MOTHERHOOD

I was first diagnosed with ADHD when I was 21. I was struggling to focus in certain areas at university, but I didn't believe ADHD was a real condition adults could have—just young, hyperactive boys. The medication I was prescribed helped me get through my degree, and then I didn't think much more about ADHD . . . until 14 years later when I became a mother. In many ways, motherhood turned out to be different from what I had imagined.

Tasks that require executive functioning (like getting ready for the day) were already more of a challenge for me than for the average person, and adding another small human into the mix interrupted all the systems I'd put in place over the years. I'd go to playgroup and forget things like baby wipes, then feel so bad having to ask the other mothers if I could borrow them. When the other parents shared their trials and tribulations, I noticed they were different from the things I struggled with. I started worrying . . .

"Do people think I'm responsible enough to look after this child?"

Looking after someone else all day and putting my needs second meant that I would be pretty dysregulated by the end of the day. After my little one had gone to bed each night and I could drop the "mask," I'd often spiral into anxiety. I would hyperfocus on really specific things around my children's health and worry all the time that they were getting a mysterious disease.

When our son turned two, he started exhibiting ADHD symptoms, and in researching and hyperfocusing on how to help him, I decided to go back to a psychiatrist for myself. I now have meds that help me with things like packing baby bags and organizing clothes, but the biggest shift has been normalizing my brain. I don't feel like I have a disability but rather a variability, as my ADHD makes some things harder but other things easier.

I'm no longer ashamed to let some unimportant things slide and lean into other stuff I know I'm amazing at, like engaging with my children's creative minds. I'm kinder to myself again and realize that I have different strengths and different weaknesses from the average person, and that's okay. As a parent, I've realized that loving and showing up for your kids is all that really matters. A forgotten library bag here or there doesn't matter when they know that they're the center of your world.

ADHD and parenthood

When ADHDers become parents, we find the masking strategies we relied on no longer hold up and our ADHD symptoms suddenly escalate. Common traits like sensitivity to noises, smells and mess can have us feeling close to the breaking point . . . frequently. In order to regulate our nervous system, we need lower-stimulation environments, but babies and children are, let's just say . . . not exactly low-stim. Hello, fight-or-flight response!

With the necessary practical tasks like cooking and cleaning being prioritized, it's really easy to put your needs second, compounding the sleep deprivation, organization stress and sensory overload. And realistically there's no removing yourself from that environment to get a (much-needed) break. Parenthood is also more challenging if your child has ADHD—about a one in two chance!

You may feel like a dysregulated hot mess a lot of the time, but remember that you have a unique ability: you deeply understand sensory overload, emotional intensity and interest-based nervous systems. This lived experience is invaluable because it means you can better help your child understand themselves, the world and the people around them.

While I'd need a whole book to really do justice to the realities of ADHD and parenthood, here are a few ideas to help you find some calm in the sensory storm today.

Sensory breaks for tired ADHD parents:

Establish daily quiet times/zones around the house to ensure everyone gets a break.

Play with modelling clay or sand or fold origami—these things help soothe parents' nervous systems too.

Use headphones (for yourself or for your kids) to listen to an audiobook or music.

Teach your kids to do breathwork to calm down (keep it simple: for example, exhale longer than you inhale).

Get out into nature with the kids and reset/recharge with a walk, a visit to a playground or "wild space" play.

Have coffee at a friend's house, and chat while your kids play together.

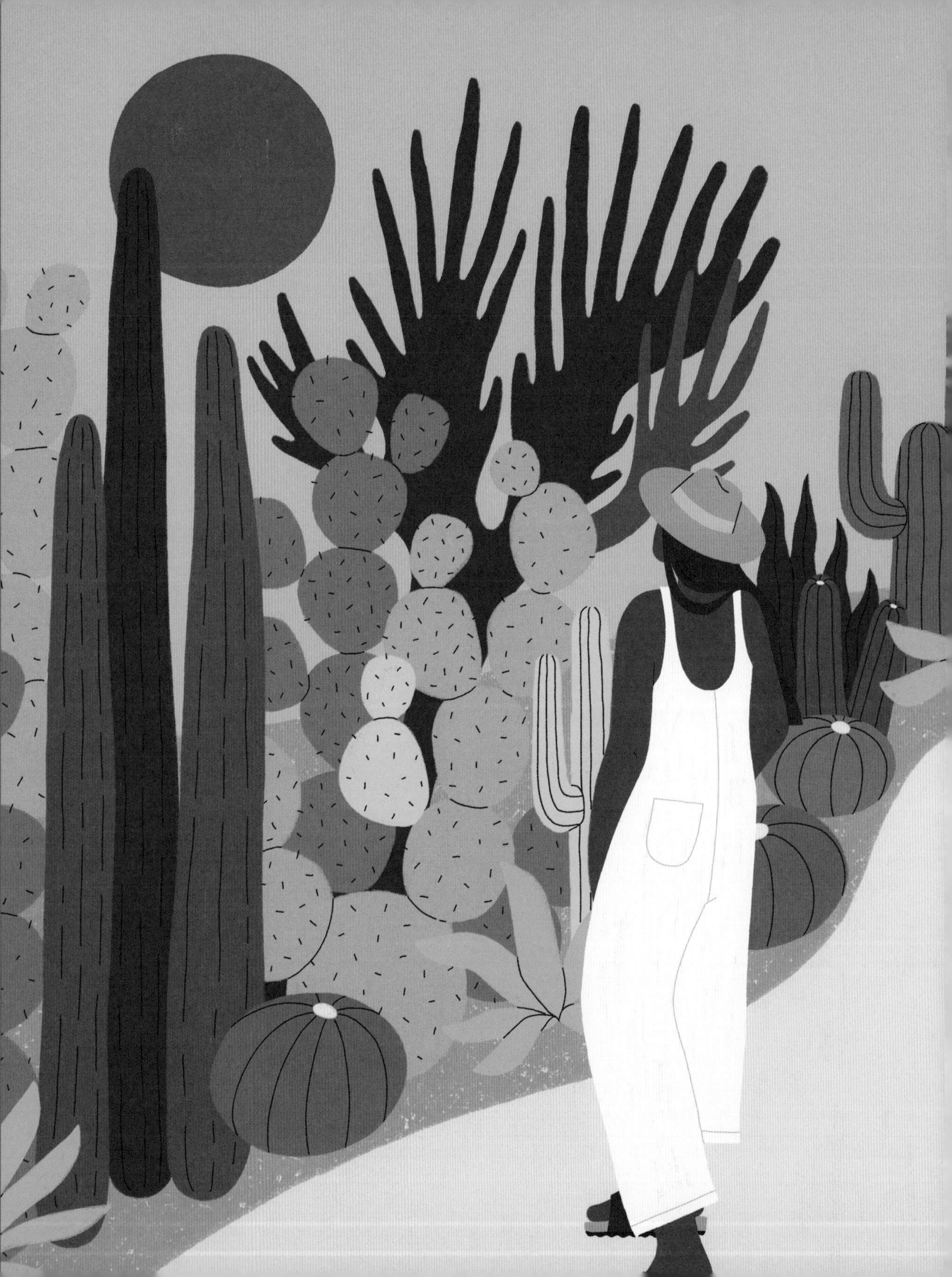

Goal Setting Re-imagined

When we talk about goals and productivity, all kinds of squirmy feelings can come up for ADHDers. We can envision a long list of goals that once excited us but now lay abandoned and long forgotten. We can pine for the big dreams that set our soul on fire, but we feel we'll never actually give it a good crack because we're so scared of failure (thanks, RSD!). Goal setting is deeply personal, so this section offers a reframe and a chance to approach this topic with curiosity.

Goals: the struggle is real

Have you ever got excited about a new project or goal, and then just as quickly got overwhelmed by the huge to-do list, hundreds of what-ifs and the fear of failing? Setting and achieving goals can be challenging for ADHDers. Things like getting organized, breaking down tasks, managing timelines and staying motivated can feel like the hardest thing on earth. But our biggest roadblock when it comes to goals is that we're so interested in everything, we tend to change goals all the time or can't choose what to focus on.

In this book, when I talk about goals, I'm also talking about habits, projects, career ambitions, personal desires, plans and intentions. We often use these words interchangeably, so I'll use the word "goal" here.

It's cruel, really, that the very nature of what it takes to achieve goals interferes with the biggest challenges we face as ADHDers . . .

We're taught that working towards goals requires:	• being organized • prioritizing and breaking down into small steps • the ability to do distasteful or boring things before rewards • working towards timelines and deadlines • fighting distractions • sustaining motivation to work towards tasks • high tolerance for low-dopamine tasks • achieving certain goals at certain times • emotional stability, instead of highs and lows • focused instead of scattered attention • forcing ourselves when our willpower fails us

There's only one thing worse than the feeling of being disorganized, forgetful and time-blind . . . the shame and frustration of a long list of half-finished projects—and nothing to show for it.

Above all, know you're not alone in feeling this way, and it's not your fault. When we talk about productivity and achieving our goals, what **doesn't** get discussed is how **heartbreaking** it is to find this process hard—because we're passionate, creative, empathetic people with a lot to give. There's a grief in not contributing in the way we hope.

Our skills and gifts are needed in this world. Because our passions can blaze through with such intensity, they can burn us (and everyone around us). Past experience makes us worry we don't have the sticking power to see projects through. I'm here to show you there's another way to look at things.

What's holding you back?

When I asked my community to share some of the things holding them back from pursuing their goals, these were a few of the themes that came up:

Getting stuck over-analyzing

Not enough time

Fear of failure

Imposter syndrome

Rejection sensitive dysphoria (RSD)

Lacking energy to persevere

Reluctant to draw attention to myself

Fear of the unknown

Waste of time, money + resources

Not feeling good enough

Unsure of where to start

No support system

Self-limiting beliefs

Shame avoidance

These responses were submitted privately, and what struck me was the thread of pain and shame that wove through each of these words. It's clear we neuro-divergents carry a burden of grief and frustration—both individually and collectively—when it comes to taking action on our deepest desires and passions. I share this to reiterate that **you're not alone** in the spiraling thoughts that intrude in the middle of the night. This book is an invitation to loosen your grip a little, activate your curiosity and explore what's holding you back, without fear of judgement or rejection.

Goals quiz

Explore your own history with goals and the choices you make about what to pursue. There are no right answers and no scores! This is just a chance for you to check in with yourself and notice some patterns in your own life.

My history with goals: a self-reflection quiz

○ I have so many goals in my brain at any one time.

○ I have a lack of clarity on what I want—I change my mind so often.

○ I don't know which goals to choose.

○ I accumulate goals, and then put them off so I have a huge backlog, and no time for any of them.

○ I overcommit, then I get overwhelmed and don't make progress on any goals.

○ I feel like I only have goals that will please others (like my parents or teachers).

○ I find it hard to organize myself and my goals.

○ I have executive dysfunction when it comes to practically executing my goals.

○ I don't write my goals down and I forget (or I do write them down and forget!).

○ I struggle to break my goals down into achievable chunks.

○ I get overwhelmed when I look at my list of ambitions.

○ Refining my goals into something tangible and realistic is hard.

○ I have clear goals, but I'm too scared to put myself out there and get rejected.

○ I have a fear of disappointing those closest to me if I fail to reach my goals.

○ I don't tell people my ambitions because I don't want them to know if I failed.

○ I get RSD (rejection sensitive dysphoria) when I don't meet my goals and stop trying.

○ I'm afraid of speaking publicly and getting negative feedback.

○ My parents are happy and I'm afraid of upsetting them if I change goals now.

○ I equate failure with rejection (e.g., "Failing the exam means the university has rejected me").

○ My goals don't feel achievable because I have ADHD.

○ I never achieve my goals, so I stop setting them—what's the point?

○ I have a lack of faith in myself to be able to achieve my goals.

○ The first step is easy, but I never seem to follow through.

○ The motivation immediately wears off after setting goals.

○ People don't expect me to achieve my goals—they've given up asking.

○ I can't complete a goal perfectly, so I won't try (perfectionism).

○ I have goals, but imposter syndrome keeps me from pursuing them.

○ I'm so overwhelmed by living that goals feel like too much to add right now.

○ I get demand avoidance, even if I'm the one who set the goal!

○ I have time blindness—I struggle to even imagine or plan for the future.

○ There are too many options and I can't choose/get overwhelmed.

Brain dump:

Well done on taking the time to reflect and be honest with yourself. Awareness is key. While there are no quick fixes, examining your deep-seated beliefs and behaviors regarding goals provides a useful foundation for re-imagining your goals, purpose and productivity. On the next page, we'll expand our thinking around goals further.

Four types of goals

I like to sort goals into four major categories, each bringing its own unique value to our lives:

Tangible goals

Tangible goals are what most people think of in relation to goals. They're things you can point to: a promotion, a graduate degree, winning a race, buying a home, a new car, receiving an award or traveling the world.

Relationship goals

These goals involve the quality of your relationships with the people you want in your life, be that a life partner or spouse, friends, family, roommates, your children, colleagues, sports team or community.

Soul goals

Soul goals are mindsets, character traits and virtues that you aspire to embody. Usually you embody soul goals through hard lessons: facing your fears, taking up space, advocating for yourself and facing setbacks.

Self-care goals

Self-care goals are about your relationship with yourself. They're process oriented, which means there is no particular end point to arrive at (e.g., nutrition, skincare, creativity, play, exercise, sleep or therapy).

There's more to life than just achieving tangible goals. How do you feel thinking about goals in this multidimensional way?

<u>Permission slips</u>

You don't always need a <u>formal goal</u> in order to be motivated to engage in learning or do an activity.

A formal goal and step-by-step process doesn't automatically imbue an activity with more <u>value.</u>

Exploring, drifting, playing and following your nose wherever it leads you are all <u>valid forms of productivity.</u>

Uncover your goals

When you're unsure about your goals, start by exploring your interests, passions and values. Reflect on what truly excites you, and seek inspiration from the experiences of others who share your values. Try a variety of activities and hobbies to see what you're passionate about—because then motivation will flow more easily. Be flexible and open to adjusting your goals as you get more data, and remember there are no "shoulds." For example, buying a house is a must for some people, but others don't want to be tied down by a mortgage. Both are valid choices!

Questions to ask yourself:

- What have you wanted to do ever since you were a kid? Are you doing it? Do you want to be?

- When have you felt most alive/uninhibited?

- Which people do you wish you had more time for?

- Do you want to live where you're living forever? Why or why not?

- Are you spending enough time resting? (Check the 10 Types of Rest guide on page 79.)

- What have you always wanted to do but been afraid to try?

- Are you feeling satisfied in your job? Do you want to explore a different job in the same career or field? Or do you want to explore another career entirely?

- What countries do you want to visit and why? How can you make that happen?

- Do you want to learn a language? Which one?

- If money was no object, what would you want to buy, invest in or experience?

- What kind of yearly salary would make life a lot easier for you and free you up to spend your time the way you want to?

- If you had a major accident that changed your life tomorrow, what would you be disappointed that you hadn't done or achieved?

- Do you want to start or continue to grow a family?

- What have you achieved that came surprisingly easy to you? Do you want to do more of that?

- What kind of challenges excite you because they're difficult and very ambitious?

My goals:

Reflect on the questions on the previous page and note down your goals here.

What are some of your existing goals?

What goals have emerged after reading the questions?

If you don't know
what your goals are . . .

Tinker, dabble and explore various hyperfixations. The more you explore and experience, the better.

Find the patterns in your hyperfixations. Your big goal is the one you can't stop thinking about, but scares the sh*t out of you.

Dare to shatter the glass and break the dream out of its perfect casing. It's got to be imperfect to be real. Prepare to be surprised.

Stuck in analysis paralysis

ADHD brains love being divergent and can get stuck in the brainstorming stage for so long that we never actually take action. **We enter into all-or-nothing thinking (or "emotional perfectionism") where exactly the right conditions have to be met in order for us to start something.** Our sensitivity leads to overthinking all possible scenarios, the impact of our decisions on other people and sometimes even deeper existential meaning. For some of us, choosing between color swatches to repaint our living room can take months, or even years! We're sensitive to things other people aren't, and that's okay.

Analysis paralysis is often rooted in fear of committing to one thing. Reminding ourselves that almost any decision (bar having kids) can be reversed and giving ourselves permission to change our mind can help us take **small, imperfect, messy action here and now**. Here are some other ideas that may help:

The 5 hack

When I'm really struggling to start a mundane task, I either:

- do 5 things (e.g., pick up 5 items)
- count down from 5, then begin
- limit myself to just doing it for 5 minutes and then I can stop

Use environmental cues

If you want to train your brain to be more productive, environmental cues are incredibly helpful. Playing certain music or wearing specific clothes can help you transition to tasks more easily. If you're working on a project and need to switch tasks—lighting a candle, facing a different direction or even going some- where like a cafe to co-work can all send signals to your brain that it's time to "do the thing." Repetition helps create a muscle memory when certain sounds, smells or environments are encountered.

When I walk into my office, my first thought is often "Smells like work." It doesn't register on a conscious level, but there's a particular wood varnish smell that subconsciously primes my brain for action.

Visualize the positive <u>and</u> the negative

Research shows that in order to motivate ourselves to achieve something, it's helpful to deeply visualize what it will look and feel like to accomplish that task or goal. It's often referred to as connecting to your "why," which is a personal process that looks different for everyone. When we do this, we activate our emotional centers and are able to integrate the goal as a priority in our mind.

Another strategy that helps make emotion-led visualization techniques more effective is imagining the worst-case scenario . . . what happens if you don't achieve that goal? For example, if you want to save money for retirement, imagining yourself struggling financially as an elderly person (and how uncomfortable that would be) can also motivate you to take action.

Remember that making <u>no decision</u> is still a decision.

The wisdom of procrastination

There are a million tips and hacks to coax our brains into starting or persisting, but experts rarely talk about **why** people with ADHD aren't being productive.

It's hardly surprising given that when a student isn't "performing" well at school, teachers and parents are quick to penalize, or provide strategies and supports, but they rarely ask why a student isn't productive. And even when they do, society just doesn't have the common language to explore different neurotypes, learning styles and the almost certain cognitive dissonance (when actions don't match intentions). Many students don't know how to articulate why they're unmotivated; they just say "I dunno." After spending many years as students in the education system, we internalize this approach and often neglect to ask ourselves why we're procrastinating.

We either punish and criticize ourselves, or we simply get addicted to finding more productivity hacks. We convince ourselves that if we just find the right tool, we'll unlock single-minded determination, enduring consistency and finally "reach our potential."

Productivity and procrastination are two sides of the same coin. We can't talk about productivity without mentioning procrastination. And we can't discuss procrastination without talking about the **wisdom of procrastination**.

Cognitive dissonance is . . .	the mental conflict when our external actions or goals don't align with our beliefs, values and authentic self-expression.

Resistance roadblocks

Procrastination gets a pretty bad rap, and yet I see procrastination as incredibly important and illuminating in doing our best work.

At its core, a lot of our procrastination is resistance. Part of us wants to move ahead with a goal, but other (louder) parts are pumping the brakes because they don't have all the information, security or emotional reassurance they need. I call these resistance roadblocks. I believe procrastination occurs because we have inner conflict we haven't been able to clearly articulate, and unspoken questions that we haven't found sufficient answers to yet.

All the back-and-forth thoughts in our brain end up like a painful internal tug-of-war, and since we're conditioned to run away from pain, the result is denial and analysis paralysis. When we realize that procrastination is an invitation to ask questions and get clarity, we don't have to stick our heads in the sand anymore. Nothing is wrong with us—in fact, procrastination can demonstrate that we are thinking critically about our situation!

Isn't procrastination just boredom?

But, I hear you say, it's not that I'm dealing with unspoken concerns, it's that I've lost my passion for this project and I'm bored. That's why I'm procrastinating. If you have ADHD, you will know the true psychological pain of being bored, so much so that the pain becomes physical.

We feel inner conflict when we're bored with a relationship or project and feel obligated or bound by society's rules to persist with it. Maybe we want to quit our tedious job, but it pays well and we need to keep saving for a house. We love our kids, but sometimes being home with toddlers is mentally understimulating to the point of being physically painful. When we admit we're bored of finger painting and picture books, we feel like terrible parents (personal experience here). Whether guilt or something else, this inner conflict can result in procrastination.

In the prevailing wisdom of the productivity industry, procrastination is a big no-no, but in many cases procrastination in ADHDers is a very important signal. It can indicate that we are, in fact, overwhelmed, burnt out and misaligned. Our bodies and brains are resisting our to-do list because they're too tired to cooperate any longer.

If you're delaying sending an email or making lunch, maybe it is just simple procrastination. But ADHDers are sensitive thinkers, and procrastination can be a sign of deeper dissatisfaction and cognitive dissonance about how our lives are turning out.

We might experience procrastination if we're ...	• Not happy or passionate about our job or career • Anxious about relationship issues or other circumstances • Unable to find hobbies or interests that inspire us • Overwhelmed and overburdened by tedious obligations • Exhausted and burnt out working or caring for others

What procrastination signals

It is my firm belief that our ADHD nervous systems have a deep and core need to be challenged creatively and to do something that lights us up. We may get physically sick if we don't do this. We also have very real needs to be understimulated, undisturbed and in a quiet space.

I've learned that procrastination is a form of resistance that signals I'm out of alignment and not getting my basic neurological needs met.

If I said I was going to find a new job but have been procrastinating, it could be because I haven't had enough solitude, space and time to think about what I really want and need. In many cases, when we can think honestly about our inner conflicts and resolve some of those, our minds start to be challenged again and we regain passion and vitality.

**Procrastination is
a form of resistance
that signals:
"I'm out of alignment
and not getting my
basic neurological
needs met."**

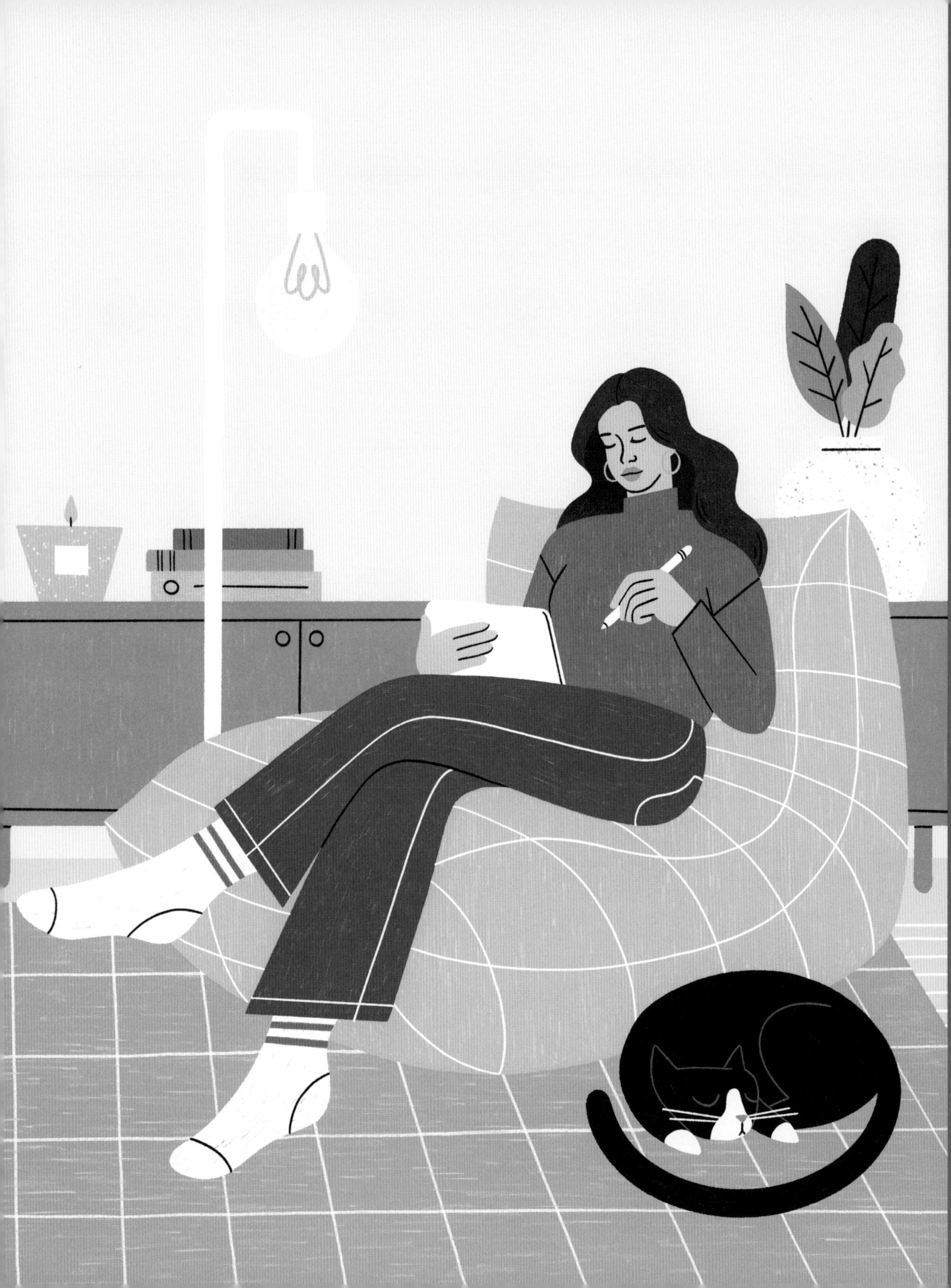

Demand avoidance

Have you avoided tasks like cleaning, going to the dentist, filling out forms and submitting timesheets? ADHD folks are famous for demand avoidance: the withering and fading of motivation under the schedules and agendas of others who want something from us. ADHDers are particularly prone to it (though it's not exclusive to ADHD). I believe that demand avoidance is hugely misunderstood.

Life as a responsible adult requires that we regularly muster the motivation to do boring tasks we don't like. This is particularly difficult for people with ADHD because we have a heightened core need for freedom. The obligations of the adult world often feel constricting for us, and we long to make decisions that are authentic.

Research conducted over the past 15 years suggests that for ADHDers, higher levels of control, meaning and freedom are crucial for well-being, motivation, happiness and executive functioning.

Therefore, if we experience a lot of demand avoidance, it could be because we unconsciously resent our lack of choice and control over our daily lives. A 2020 study on unmotivated college students with ADHD revealed that a lack of autonomy was a constant source of frustration for them. Another research paper found that chronic unmet autonomy needs led to feelings of helplessness and emotional dysfunction.

ADHDers have a vital need for independence

These scientific findings are rooted in a truth that's been obvious to the ADHD community for a long time. We have a deep and valid need to be autonomous, and explore what excites us, which will change on any given day. This isn't a luxury or an inconvenience—on the contrary, it's a necessity if we want to be healthy and fulfilled. Our need for self-direction is an insistent, inherent part of who we are. When we're empowered, this autonomy can be a huge asset to us and those around us.

If demand avoidance is our protest against the imposed agendas of people and societal structures, isn't the antidote to demand avoidance *doing more of what we actually want to do?* Could it be that demand avoidance is a sign we aren't allowing ourselves the conditions to sprawl in the sun, chase after our passions (however trivial they may seem) and be curious, playful and creative?

I've found in my own life that when I block out time in the calendar to daydream, read poetry and write, my core needs as a neurodivergent get met. It feels almost rebellious to do so, but—bit by bit—my tolerance for doing the obligatory, low-dopamine tasks increases. No, I'll never be a domestic goddess or enjoy doing my taxes. But exercising uncompromising control over some aspects of my life gives me more energy to do the boring, essential tasks.

Which begs the question: What do you really want to do, and are you doing it? If you're not, is it any wonder you have rampant demand avoidance?

I'm not naively suggesting you stick it to the man and quit so you can pursue your passions full-time, because life often isn't that simple. But I am inviting you to step outside our classic ADHD "all-or-nothing thinking" on this issue and explore some gentle middle ground.

Some ideas you could try:

✳ Book 6 hours in the calendar every second Saturday to hyperfocus undisturbed.

✳ Budget for an overnight "creative/soul retreat" at a local Airbnb once every three months.

✳ Consider reducing your workweek to four days, as having Fridays to tinker in a quiet house is essential for your mental well-being. If the four-day schedule doesn't cover the rent or mortgage, consider the benefits of downsizing your home.

✳ Keep working full-time, but choose to spend two weeks of your holiday leave working on your passion project/side hustle, instead of going away on vacation. For ADHDers, working on passion projects can feel more rejuvenating than lying on a beach.

Seasons of adversity

In a discussion about core needs and freedom, it's important to mention that there are tough seasons of life when our autonomy can be stripped from us—be it the need to care for young children, family members with illness or specific care needs, aging parents, our own illness, or during seasons of financial hardship, life upheaval or natural disaster. If that's you, I see you. In these times, it may be difficult to imagine how you could live your life by design; you're taking it day by day, hour by hour—sometimes breath by breath.

"Doing what you really want to be doing" is an ideal that may not be possible for you right now, but when this season ends (this too shall pass), exploring your own self-expression again will be a crucial part of healing. You deserve that right—it's an essential need, not a luxury.

Your thoughts

What are some of your core autonomy needs? How could you meet them?

Break up the tension by dancing or doing somatic movement. You don't need to be a good dancer—just swaying, squatting and moving your arms is a great start for releasing muscle tension.

Unleash pent-up thoughts and unblock your flow with free writing (writing without stopping). If you don't know what to write, write "I don't know what to write" over and over, until you do. This doesn't need to make sense and you can burn it after if you want.

Final ideas for that _stuck_ feeling:

Try a simple breathwork practice called the physiological sigh. This is when you intentionally take a deep breath in and let it out in a long, satisfying sigh. Let your shoulders fall and feel the stress leave your body and face. Repeat 3 times.

Create a _private_ Instagram or other social media account where you can record yourself talking about your goals. The idea is to have a space you can quickly share without losing the video files. You can also record into voice notes on your phone.

Your thoughts

Reframe the moment you get stuck as one of the **best gifts productivity can give you**. It can reveal valuable insights and help you course correct. Write down the behaviors you experience with analysis paralysis, procrastination and demand avoidance. When you're more aware of these patterned behaviors, you can interrupt them to reflect and look at your situation with curiosity.

What might analysis paralysis be telling you?

What wisdom does procrastination hold?

What can you learn from your demand avoidance?

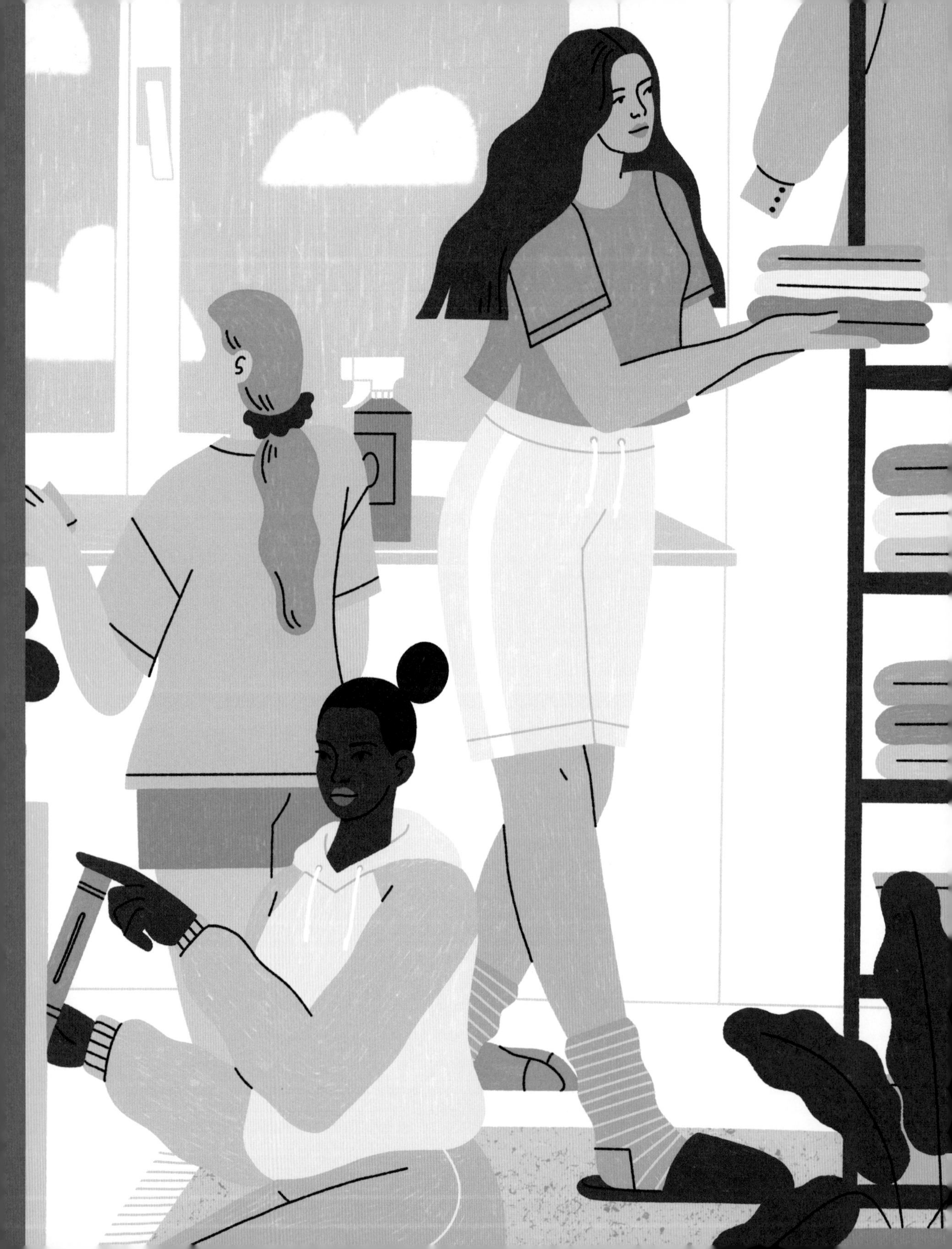

Body doubling

"Body doubling" is a term used in the ADHD community to describe the act of working alongside someone else in a way that increases your productivity. A body double can be a friend or family member who acts as an external motivator, anchor or grounding presence to help you stay on task. They don't need to be working on the same task, or even the same room—you can body double using video chat or specific body doubling websites.

Tasks you can do with a body double:

Self care + hygiene

Brushing teeth, showering, exercising, skincare, meditation, walking

Shopping + making meals

Choosing recipes, grocery shopping, meal prep, cleaning up, recycling

Life admin + work/study

Taxes, working/studying, researching, prioritizing, delegating, backing up files

Household tasks

Cleaning, tidying, mowing the lawn, decluttering, moving house

Your thoughts

Which tasks do you struggle with, and who could you body double with?

Hyperfocus

"Hyperfocus" (the verb) or "hyperfixation" (the noun) describes the state of extreme immersive focus on a project or special interest, where the outside world and all responsibilities melt away. It's a familiar feeling … something has piqued your curiosity and you impulsively follow it down the rabbit hole. It may take the form of intense research or an unplanned 8-hour binge-watching session. Sometimes a hyperfixation develops into a full-blown innovation that you simply must bring to life. For ADHDers, it almost feels like an emotional pull towards the thing of interest, and if we're interrupted (or unable to continue), it can physically or emotionally hurt.

Hyperfocus is a commonly reported trait of ADHD. One 2021 study associated hyperfocus with improvements in task performance, but there's still a lack of scientific research on hyperfocus and ADHD. A lot can be learned from other findings though, such as studies on a related phenomenon known as "flow state," or research linking emotions like curiosity to enhanced attention, learning and memory. In a 2017 study, researchers suggested that dopamine helps with learning by strengthening the connections between brain cells, making it more likely the information will be stored in long-term memory.

When ADHDers enter a state of hyperfocus, we are highly stimulated and "locked-in." I suspect that finding a new hyperfixation that we're excited about gives our ADHD brains a big hit of dopamine (and other chemicals). That surge of dopamine means we can often learn a vast amount about a new topic or skill in a short period of time, retain that knowledge and make connections to it.

Since stimulation is the highest priority for an ADHD brain, we lose track of time and ignore more mundane needs and responsibilities like eating, using the bathroom or drinking water. But on the positive side, the same 2021 study found that during hyperfocus, ADHD individuals also lose "reflective self-consciousness." Losing self-consciousness gave them the ability to create and act without self-judgement, which is where most of the magic happens.

The dopamine from our latest hyperfixation will sustain us for a while, until the boredom sets in. Once we lose interest, our previous obsession can feel like the most boring thing in the world (#DeadToMe). People with ADHD can then end up in a "hyperfocus cycle."

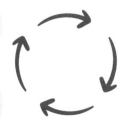

Lock eyes on a new shiny hyperfixation

Spend many hours or days on your hyperfixation

Get bored with your hyperfixation

Lose track of time and ignore your needs

Long-haul flights

When we work on projects that align with our goals and values and use our hyperfocus ability as "rocket fuel," the results can be remarkable. Hyperfocus can be hard to imagine if you don't have ADHD, so I developed an analogy called the long-haul flight to describe what it feels like mentally and physically.

Four stages of hyperfocus: the long-haul flight

1 **Taxiing on the runway: Waiting mode**

ADHDers are always on the lookout for new sources of stimulation, and this is when we're taxiing on the runway. We can feel quite agitated in this stage.

2 **Takeoff: Unstoppable speed**

Finally! Our curiosity is piqued, our coordinates are set and we suddenly gather speed and take off, ready to soar into hyperfocus. It's very hard to slow us down in takeoff.

3 **Flight mode: Hyperfocus**

We're cruising at altitude, covering a huge distance in a matter of hours. Interruptions can feel cataclysmic, and being diverted (pulled out of hyperfocus) is very stressful.

4 **Landing: Coming out of hyperfocus**

We end hyperfocus sessions like a plane descending from 30,000 feet . . . Our attention becomes shallow, we ease out and finally we're done. I often feel jet-lagged after a hyperfocus session.

The fear of losing the "spark"

There's something deeper at the heart of our constant revolving door of new hyperfixations, and I think it looks like a kind of grief. Evidence shows that ADHD brains have dysregulated dopamine reward pathways. When dopamine stores are flagging, new hyperfixations offer fresh dopamine sources—shiny objects are a biological need for us. We fall in love with a new project, and for an ADHDer it really is like falling in love hard and fast. For a while our new hyperfixation is all we can think and talk about. "This time it feels different," we think.

The grief of fading excitement

Let's talk about the unspoken grief we experience when that initial surge of excitement begins to fade. It seems trivial, so we don't have language for this kind of grief, but it's like a version of falling out of love.

Not all hyperfixations hold the same weight. If we're merely sick of the sour watermelon slushie we binged every day on our commute home last week, we'll probably be okay. However, certain passions carry deeper significance for us. There's a sense of grief that accompanies the repeated loss of interest in something we were once deeply committed to—be it a career path, friendship, degree, side hustle, hobby or renovation project.

As we quit projects time and time again, we begin to withdraw, growing more hesitant and skeptical of our own intuition. **We don't want to truly commit to starting something <u>because</u> it means so much to us**. It's not unlike relationship commitment phobia. If you've been burned, you might struggle to get past two dates. When you meet someone special, you quickly self-sabotage because you want to avoid the pain of a breakup down the track. You've got too much to lose. We can do the same thing with dreams that matter a great deal to us.

We keep our biggest goals at arm's length because we don't know if we'll survive the potential failure—having our dream shattered only weeks or months after we've begun. We'd rather hedge our bets and hold on to a dream. While they're locked in our imagination, our dreams are perfect.

When we move to take action, our dreams exist in the real world, and that means they'll be imperfect. They'll change. They might disappoint us. But they could also surprise us, and change our lives beyond what we ever could have hoped.

We lose so much when we play defensively like this. We miss the opportunity to fall in love with and nurture a lifelong passion. We miss the chance to show ourselves we are capable of making great things. We live a life full of regrets and what-ifs, wishing we'd taken a chance.

One thing is for sure—if our goals stay locked in our minds because we're afraid to fail, nothing will happen. If we let go of fear and chase our goals, they'll evolve and change, but **something will <u>happen.</u>**

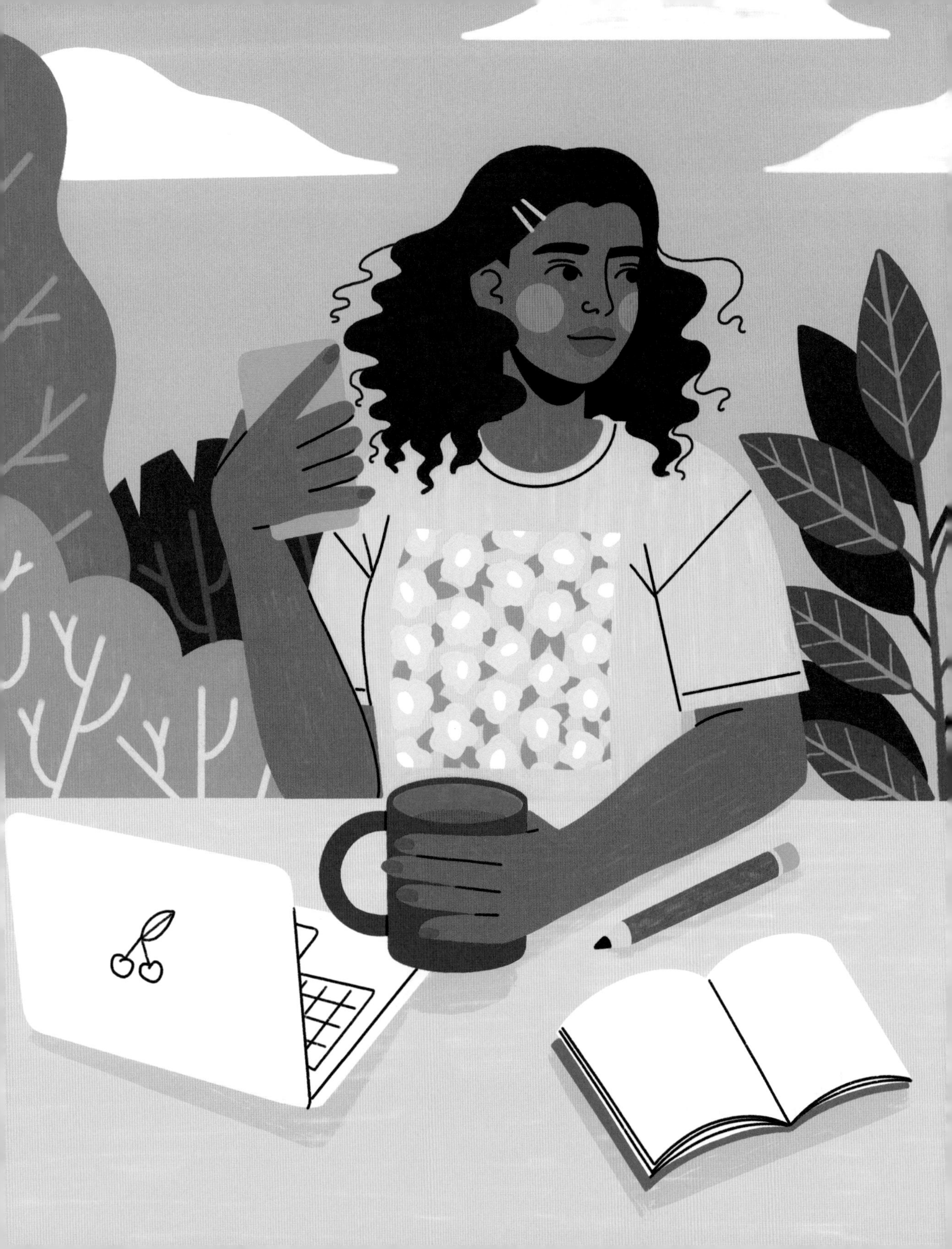

Self-talk traps that can choke our natural ADHD creativity and curiosity . . .

"I need to be perfect at this right away."

"It needs to look exactly how I envisaged."

"If it's not perfect, it's a complete failure and waste of time."

Having high standards and a clear vision of our dreams means that we quickly become intimidated by the size of our goals.

Why we get overwhelmed

To paraphrase Oscar Wilde, "some things are too important to be taken seriously." ADHDers take our goals and ambitions very seriously; we care deeply and are often quite perfectionistic. Because of this emotional intensity, we tend to tie the worth of a project to its outcome. If we don't achieve what we're imagining, then it's a failure. Reframing productivity can look like relaxing our grip on the outcome, and being more curious and playful as we're pursuing goals.

When we're interested in something, ADHDers have curiosity, creativity and initiative in bucketloads, but we tie ourselves up in knots with our impatience ("I need to be perfect at this right away"), imagination ("It needs to look exactly how I envisaged") and rigid thinking ("If it's not perfect, it's a complete failure and waste of time").

Having high standards and a clear vision of our dreams means that we quickly become intimidated by the size of our goals. It feels like there's so much at stake, because for us—there is. **When working on a creative project, I typically feel exasperated and agitated, because it means so much to me; I so badly want to conceptualize it in a way that "does it justice."** I get impatient to see that result, and I also wrestle with the pain that I'm not there yet.

I've realized that I have a certain threshold for things that matter to me most. I can work on something for a few days, and then I get frustrated (at the same time, it's likely the dopamine is wearing off) and quit with dramatic final words. But within a day or two, I'm champing at the bit for another challenge, or back fiddling with the project I abandoned.

ADHDers tend to feel overwhelmed when imagining a goal, because we see all the stages of a project happening at once. Our time blindness means we see outside time. It's like time collapses, and everything is either happening either now or never. Before we know it, our brain has taken off like a bolting horse.

Being able to see a big vision and race ahead imagining all the components is a valuable gift. This is the only way ADHD folks know how to be, so we assume that everyone has this ability, but they don't. Because we see the whole instead of the small parts, we feel overwhelmed by how much there is to do, and this can mean we struggle to keep going (or start at all). Holding on for dear life takes energy, and a lot of us just slip off the horse and pick smaller goals that our brain doesn't bolt towards.

There's certainly a time for doing less, and taking it easy. But my instinct says that ADHDers are healthiest when we're chasing sparkly, ambitious, so-big-it-scares-us goals.

If we recognize that our visionary abilities are often a sought-after skill, we can partner with people (often neurotypicals) who are incredibly good at taking a big vision and managing the smaller steps. I'd hazard a guess that the ADHDers who've become successful have worked out that they need that methodical person in their life. I'd be lost without my husband, who runs the practical side of our business. We're a team, working together to bring projects to life.

Bernice's story

LATE DIAGNOSIS AND CULTURAL STIGMA

For years, I struggled with the frustration and shame of being different from my peers. I'm from Hong Kong, and in my family of origin and culture, there was a lot of stigma around ADHD. Most people thought of it as a sickness or a problem that needed to be fixed, rather than a natural part of human diversity. This made it difficult for me to seek out resources, as I felt like I was doing something wrong.

Having ADHD in a world that doesn't fully understand or support divergent ways of thinking and being essentially harms our sense of self, and limits our potential.

As a child and teen, I often found it challenging to focus in class, as my mind would wander to other things. I also had intrusive thoughts that made it hard to concentrate on the task at hand, and sometimes I had to stifle the urge to act out because I wanted to seem more normal." Most of the time, I had trouble sitting still for long periods and would fidget or get up and move around.

Getting diagnosed at 26 was a game changer. It allowed me to embrace my unique strengths and quirks and develop strategies to manage my symptoms. I'm now more productive and focused on my goals, recognizing when I need to take a break or push myself a little harder. I love to keep making small amounts of progress. I do monthly, quarterly and yearly reviews with the Future ADHD planner to make sure that my actions are aligned with my purposes in the best way possible. I've also found a community of like-minded neurodivergents, which has allowed me to share my experiences, learn from others and feel seen in ways I never have before.

My neurodivergent brain gives me a unique perspective on the world and means I'm able to approach problems in unconventional ways. I love the creativity, hyperfocus and the depth of my feelings.

When I'm passionate about something, I become fully immersed in it and can't help but think about it all the time. This can be both a blessing and a curse, as it can sometimes make it hard to focus on other things, but it also means that I have a lot of enthusiasm and energy for the things that matter to me.

ADHD is more about a loss of interest and motivation than a lack of attention and concentration.

Too many ideas, can't choose

Learning the difference between divergent and convergent thinking helped me realize I spend most of my time in divergent thinking mode. Suddenly I understood why I would get an idea, jump straight into a flurry of brainstorming and then become overwhelmed and exit stage left. I was swimming in possibility, but this didn't help—it caused analysis paralysis.

Dr. Tamara Rosier explains that children have a natural capacity for divergent thinking, but by adulthood, most neurotypical brains are comfortable in convergent thinking mode. Both convergent and divergent thinking are important, but when we use one more than the other, we can get stuck on goals and projects, either at the ideation phase or the execution phase.

"Divergent thinkers have possibility brains," Dr. Rosier says. "Their minds naturally explore and elaborate on ideas, examining what could be."

When it comes to goals, projects and ideas, ADHD brains have a tendency to stay stuck in the divergent-thinking brainstorm stage way too long. Why? Because it delivers opportunities for novelty, experimentation and imagination—things our minds love. Exploring a new idea is important, but to meet our goals, we need to move to the taking-action phase before we lose interest. That's where those (dreaded) convergent thinking skills come in.

You might be wondering—"Huh? What is convergent thinking?"

We use convergent thinking to plan the action steps to achieve our goal (after the blue-sky brainstorming phase). Working towards a goal with clarity requires logic, prioritizing and persistence. It might sound boring, but divergent thinking imagines wonderful possibilities and convergent thinking actually brings those dreams to life. They are both crucial steps.

The Div/Con Planning template

The following template Div/Con Planning is a framework I developed that will help you find a balance between divergent and convergent thinking. Describe a clear goal that you can visualize and "feel" when you close your eyes, because this increases your motivation. Set a time limit on how long you'll spend in divergent thinking mode, and when you'll move to convergent thinking. Convergent thinking may tire you out but body doubling can help (see page 111). Keep reminding yourself of your goal and visualize yourself enjoying it to keep your brain on track. This may feel mechanical at first because it's unnatural for you—remember that each time you practice, your neural pathways get stronger.

TIP: If you're struggling, try the Color to Calm exercises in the Take 10, Every 10 pages. They help transition your brain from divergent to convergent thinking.

Div/Con Planning

Try this template for yourself on page 222.

1. OUTCOME/GOAL/MY "WHY":

Be descriptive, and visualize how you'll feel.

Plan a holiday somewhere warm where I can relax and switch off from work.

I want to zone out, eat delicious food and read a good book.

2. DIVERGENT THINKING BRAINSTORM:

Set a time limit on divergent thinking.

TIME LIMIT! 2 MINS/HRS

Bali for a diving trip

That sound-healing retreat my colleague went to in Arizona

Do I want friends to come or go alone? Need to find a friend who wants the same kind of holiday as me

The Maldives?? Too expensive

Cheap flights to Spain <u>but</u> I want to do Barcelona when I have the energy to be a tourist. So maybe not for this type of holiday

Resort style so I can eat out and not have to cook vs. Airbnb with kitchen?

3. MY DECISION: Resort in Bali where I can stay by the pool all day

4. CONVERGENT THINKING TASK LIST:

What practical steps do I need to take that will help me achieve my goal?

☐ Budget based on priorities, my "why"

☐ Find an all-inclusive resort package

☐ Request time off work

☐ Book by April 15

☐ Research flights

☐ Book airport transfer

☐ Organize house sitter

☐ Find passport

☐ Change money

☐ Pack bags

If you get lost and feel tempted to slip back into divergent thinking, remember to focus on your goal, visualize how you want to feel and use that positive feeling to create actionable steps and stay on track. Your future self will thank you.

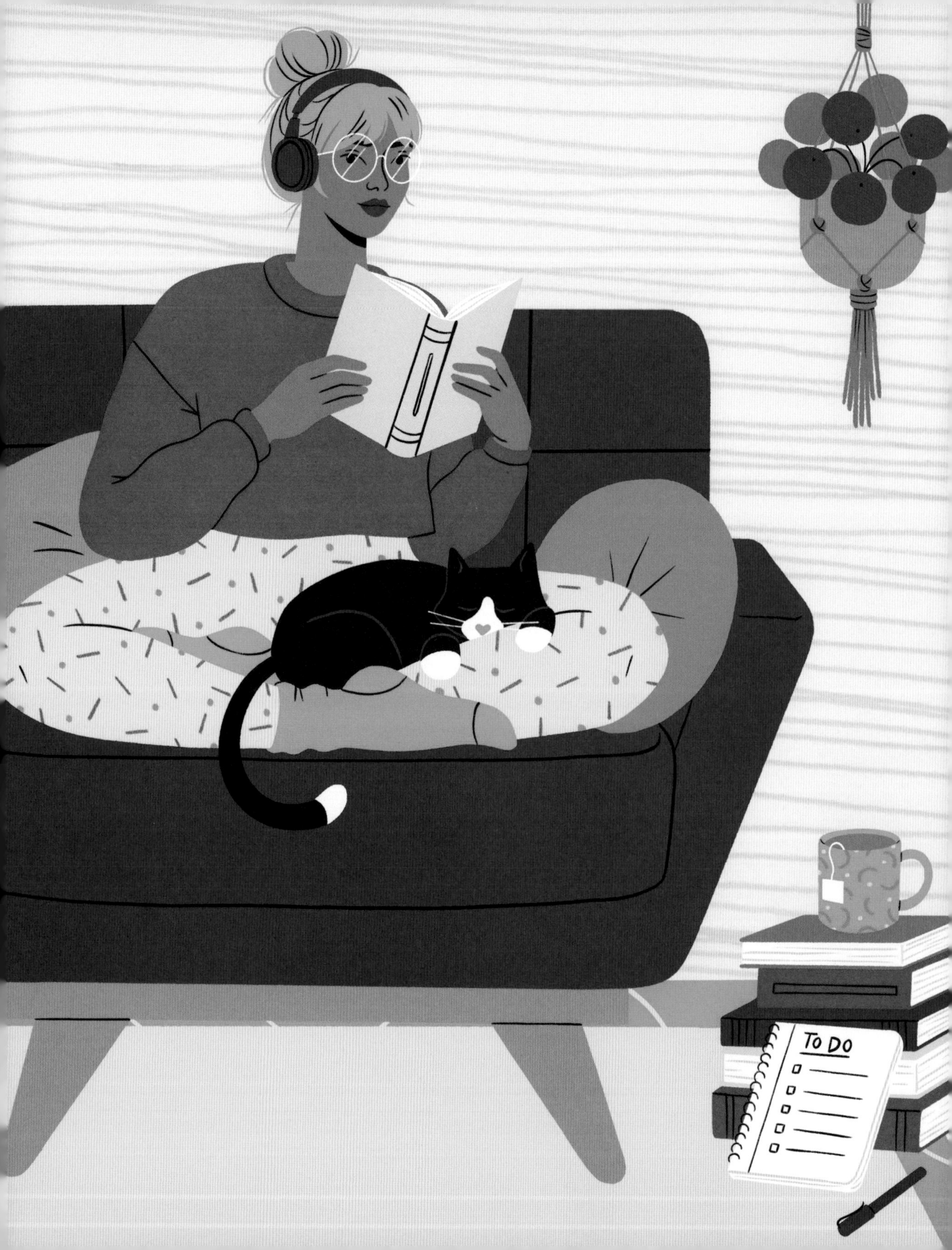
TO DO

The Daily Focus Friend

The Daily Focus Friend pages are low-demand, flexible, guilt-free and undated. Use them as needed; no shame if you miss a week or a month! I've designed this template based on ADHD research to help you sort through the chaos and find a quick path to clarity. I've included a two-page review every 10 pages, inviting moments of reflection and a chance to recalibrate.

Reframing productivity

Do you have a graveyard of planners, journals and diaries? Do you get two weeks in, forget a day or two and then throw it in the bin?

Let's talk about planners. A lot of ADHDers just want to be better at organizing themselves and planning, but they feel like it's an impossible task for so many reasons. Most planners are rigid systems designed for efficiency, productivity and consistency. And these are admirable qualities, for sure, but they can't be the primary motivator for a dopamine-driven ADHD brain.

With motivation alone, we can buy the pretty planner, set a great intention and write an eloquent, majestic first entry with fancy glitter pens. But then the motivation (dopamine) dies because we miss a day or week, and suddenly we're "failing." The once shiny planner repulses us as we mutter: "If it's not perfect, it's a complete failure and waste of my time" (page 116).

Throw it out. Repeat.

Again and again.

But what if I told you throwing out those other planners made complete sense? Your brain knew those systems were too rigid and so it balked. The key is, it's not the planner that works (or doesn't). It's the exhale you breathe when you learn how to unhook from self-shaming narratives and partner with your creative, inconsistent, brilliant ADHD brain.

When you have a deep understanding of yourself, and know how to regulate your emotions and nervous system, your approach to organization changes. You realize you don't have to work for your planner, but it's a tool that's meant to work for you. Which means you get to make up the rules.

When I launched the Future ADHD planner, I approached it with one question: "How do you create a tool that someone with ADHD can actually stick to?" In my research, I came to realize how important it is for us to be emotionally ready for planning.

So, I threw out the rule book. Dated pages weren't mandatory, the layout evolved with you and the planner gently nudged you to look after yourself first. I actively encouraged people to leave shame at the door, be messy and inconsistent. Instead of calling blank pages "unproductive," I just said: "You obviously didn't need it that day, and that's okay."

And people relaxed. Planning was no longer a chore and it was easy to jump back in after weeks off—without the guilt. As a result ADHDers stuck with it.

The Daily Focus Friend is a tool that has been (and continues to be) used by more than 70,000 neurodivergents, many of whom rave about its simplicity and effectiveness; I think in large part, because I encourage people to let go of the planning "shoulds."

It turns out people have always wanted to give up the stuffy "shoulds," they just needed permission. Together, let's jettison the shame that comes with being inconsistent and disorganized ("fire it into the sun," as my husband says!) and embrace our brains, our way. This book holds up a mirror, shows you where you need support and gives you the tools to get there.

So in this next section, it's time for you to use a planner . . . Scary, I know. But this time you come armed with everything you've learned in this book about yourself. There's no pressure to use it in a particular way. Just focus on making today a little more organized. Then tomorrow, and so on. Little by little, a little becomes a lot.

So let's take a quick tour . . .

The Daily Focus Friend (DFF)	We'll use dopamine rewards (see pages 38-39 for ideas) to pull ourselves through boring but necessary tasks. There's a home for all your random thoughts in the Brain Dump section (so you don't lose them). And keep an eye out for our cute self-care icons to remind you to nourish your nervous system—as a priority!
Take 10, Every 10 Reflection + Reset Page	Every 10 days (however long that takes you—there's no pressure, remember!), you'll have a chance to reflect. The Take 10, Every 10 check-ins are intentionally designed to help you celebrate your small (or big!) wins and revisit anything you might have put in the "too-hard basket." How are you feeling about those goals you set? Did you notice any glimmers this week? What's your current hyperfixation?
The Template Toolbox	On page 213, you'll find a section called The Template Toolbox dedicated to other planning templates. These pages are more specific and are there to support you when you need them. I won't give too much away— have fun exploring them yourself!

I know it seems crazy, but you **can** use a planner. It's just that every planner ever created has been made for the neurotypical brain. It's about time you experienced something uniquely suited to your neurotype, made by someone with ADHD who truly gets what it's like. Welcome to your Daily Focus Friend.

Guide: Daily Focus Friend

The time blocking spots can be made AM or PM to suit your schedule.

Color the heart in when you're done so you can quickly find your place when flicking through.

Use the self-care icons to check off tasks—color or highlight when complete.

Daily focus friend

SUN MON TUE WED THU FRI SAT
○   ○   ○   ○   ○   ○   ○

FOCUS/QUOTE:

DATE:

SELF-CARE:

TODAY - TIME BLOCKING:

5:00
6:00
7:00
8:00
9:00
10:00
11:00
12:00
1:00
2:00
3:00
4:00
5:00
6:00
7:00
8:00
9:00

BORING (BUT NECESSARY) TASKS:

01
02
03

REWARD TO MYSELF AFTER:

DON'T FORGET:

☐
☐
☐
☐
☐

PEOPLE TO RESPOND TO:

☐
☐
☐

LEAVE IT FOR LATER BRAIN DUMP:

HABIT GOAL:

DONE!
☐

129

ICON KEY

⊘ Medication

🦷 Dental care

♡ Exercise

☀ Vitamin D

🎧 Music/podcast

📝 Journal/work

🧘 Meditation

🛁 Shower

🐾 Pets/nature

📞 Phone loved ones

🥤 Hydrate

🧹 Clean

💻 Work/study

🍜 Eat a meal

Brain dump all your random thoughts here, and revisit at the end of the day, so you don't get tempted to run down a rabbit hole.

Guide: Take 10, *Every 10*

Take 10 minutes (or longer) to reflect and reset with the guided prompts across these two pages. You don't have to complete on a weekly basis, just every time you finish 10 Daily Focus Friend pages—whether that's over 10 consecutive days or stop-start over four weeks!

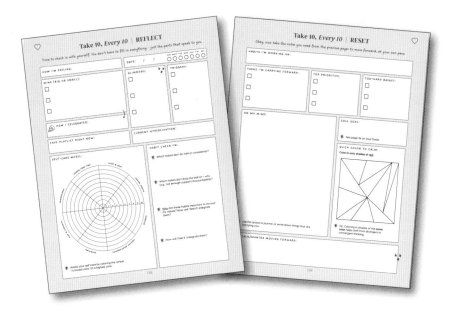

What we mean by these words

✳ *Glimmers*—small things in your day that made you smile
Triggers—moments that triggered you (build self-awareness)

✳ *Celebrate your wins*—take a photo to mark the occasion, keep a diary, share on social media, buy yourself something to represent the win

✳ *Too-hard basket*—tasks that you don't want to forget, but don't have bandwidth for right now

✳ *Quick color to calm*—a great way to move from divergent (creative) thinking to convergent (logical) thinking

✳ *Soul goal*—wins that are less tangible and more personal (e.g., being more resilient, self-kindness, reframing negative thoughts)

Daily focus friend

SUN   MON   TUE   WED   THU   FRI   SAT

○   ○   ○   ○   ○   ○   ○

FOCUS/QUOTE:

DATE:

SELF-CARE:

TODAY—TIME BLOCKING:

5:00	
6:00	
7:00	
8:00	
9:00	
10:00	
11:00	
12:00	
1:00	
2:00	
3:00	
4:00	
5:00	
6:00	
7:00	
8:00	
9:00	

BORING (BUT NECESSARY) TASKS:

01

02

03

🎉 REWARD TO MYSELF AFTER:

DON'T FORGET:

☐

☐

☐

☐

☐

PEOPLE TO RESPOND TO:

☐

☐

☐

LEAVE IT FOR LATER BRAIN DUMP:

HABIT GOAL:

DONE! ☐

Daily focus friend

FOCUS/QUOTE:

DATE:

SELF-CARE:

TODAY—TIME BLOCKING:

| 5:00 |
| 6:00 |
| 7:00 |
| 8:00 |
| 9:00 |
| 10:00 |
| 11:00 |
| 12:00 |
| 1:00 |
| 2:00 |
| 3:00 |
| 4:00 |
| 5:00 |
| 6:00 |
| 7:00 |
| 8:00 |
| 9:00 |

BORING (BUT NECESSARY) TASKS:

01

02

03

REWARD TO MYSELF AFTER:

DON'T FORGET:

☐
☐
☐
☐
☐

PEOPLE TO RESPOND TO:

☐
☐
☐

LEAVE IT FOR LATER BRAIN DUMP:

HABIT GOAL:

DONE!
☐

Daily focus friend

SUN MON TUE WED THU FRI SAT
○   ○   ○   ○   ○   ○   ○

FOCUS/QUOTE:

DATE:

SELF-CARE:

TODAY—TIME BLOCKING:

5:00

6:00

7:00

8:00

9:00

10:00

11:00

12:00

1:00

2:00

3:00

4:00

5:00

6:00

7:00

8:00

9:00

BORING (BUT NECESSARY) TASKS:

01

02

03

REWARD TO MYSELF AFTER:

DON'T FORGET:

☐

☐

☐

☐

☐

PEOPLE TO RESPOND TO:

☐

☐

☐

LEAVE IT FOR LATER BRAIN DUMP:

HABIT GOAL:

DONE!
☐

Daily focus friend

FOCUS/QUOTE:

DATE:

SELF-CARE:

TODAY—TIME BLOCKING:

5:00	
6:00	
7:00	
8:00	
9:00	
10:00	
11:00	
12:00	
1:00	
2:00	
3:00	
4:00	
5:00	
6:00	
7:00	
8:00	
9:00	

BORING (BUT NECESSARY) TASKS:

01

02

03

REWARD TO MYSELF AFTER:

DON'T FORGET:

☐

☐

☐

☐

☐

PEOPLE TO RESPOND TO:

☐

☐

☐

LEAVE IT FOR LATER BRAIN DUMP:

HABIT GOAL:

DONE!
☐

Daily focus friend

FOCUS/QUOTE:

DATE:

SELF-CARE:

TODAY—TIME BLOCKING:

5:00

6:00

7:00

8:00

9:00

10:00

11:00

12:00

1:00

2:00

3:00

4:00

5:00

6:00

7:00

8:00

9:00

BORING (BUT NECESSARY) TASKS:

01

02

03

REWARD TO MYSELF AFTER:

DON'T FORGET:

☐

☐

☐

☐

☐

PEOPLE TO RESPOND TO:

☐

☐

☐

LEAVE IT FOR LATER BRAIN DUMP:

HABIT GOAL:

DONE! ☐

Daily focus friend

FOCUS/QUOTE:

DATE:

SELF-CARE:

TODAY—TIME BLOCKING:

5:00

6:00

7:00

8:00

9:00

10:00

11:00

12:00

1:00

2:00

3:00

4:00

5:00

6:00

7:00

8:00

9:00

BORING (BUT NECESSARY) TASKS:

01

02

03

🎉 REWARD TO MYSELF AFTER:

DON'T FORGET:

☐

☐

☐

☐

☐

PEOPLE TO RESPOND TO:

☐

☐

☐

LEAVE IT FOR LATER BRAIN DUMP:

HABIT GOAL:

DONE! ☐

Daily focus friend

SUN MON TUE WED THU FRI SAT

FOCUS/QUOTE:

DATE:

SELF-CARE:

TODAY—TIME BLOCKING:

5:00	
6:00	
7:00	
8:00	
9:00	
10:00	
11:00	
12:00	
1:00	
2:00	
3:00	
4:00	
5:00	
6:00	
7:00	
8:00	
9:00	

BORING (BUT NECESSARY) TASKS:

01	
02	
03	

REWARD TO MYSELF AFTER:

DON'T FORGET:

- [ ]
- [ ]
- [ ]
- [ ]
- [ ]

PEOPLE TO RESPOND TO:

- [ ]
- [ ]
- [ ]

LEAVE IT FOR LATER BRAIN DUMP:

HABIT GOAL:

DONE!

Daily focus friend

FOCUS/QUOTE:

DATE:

SELF-CARE:

TODAY—TIME BLOCKING:

5:00	
6:00	
7:00	
8:00	
9:00	
10:00	
11:00	
12:00	
1:00	
2:00	
3:00	
4:00	
5:00	
6:00	
7:00	
8:00	
9:00	

BORING (BUT NECESSARY) TASKS:

01

02

03

REWARD TO MYSELF AFTER:

DON'T FORGET:

☐

☐

☐

☐

☐

PEOPLE TO RESPOND TO:

☐

☐

☐

LEAVE IT FOR LATER BRAIN DUMP:

HABIT GOAL:

DONE!
☐

Daily focus friend

SUN MON TUE WED THU FRI SAT
○   ○   ○   ○   ○   ○   ○

FOCUS/QUOTE:

DATE:

SELF-CARE:

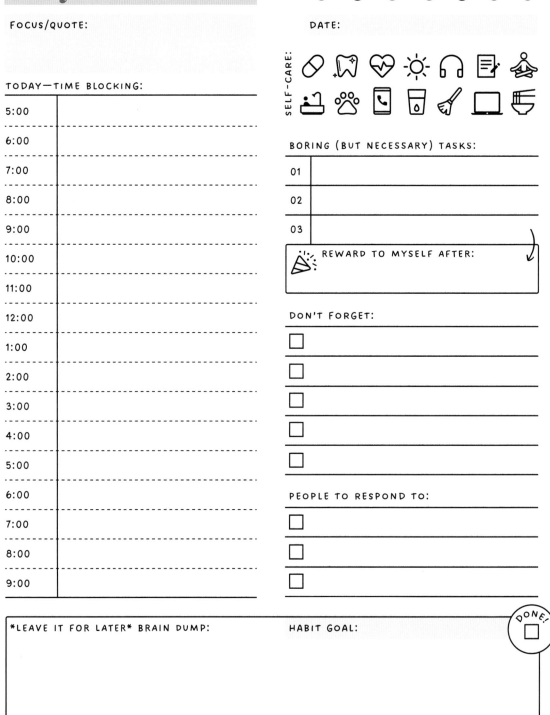

TODAY—TIME BLOCKING:

5:00

6:00

7:00

8:00

9:00

10:00

11:00

12:00

1:00

2:00

3:00

4:00

5:00

6:00

7:00

8:00

9:00

BORING (BUT NECESSARY) TASKS:

01

02

03

REWARD TO MYSELF AFTER:

DON'T FORGET:

☐

☐

☐

☐

☐

PEOPLE TO RESPOND TO:

☐

☐

☐

LEAVE IT FOR LATER BRAIN DUMP:

HABIT GOAL:

DONE!
☐

Daily focus friend

SUN MON TUE WED THU FRI SAT
○   ○   ○   ○   ○   ○   ○

FOCUS/QUOTE:

DATE:

SELF-CARE: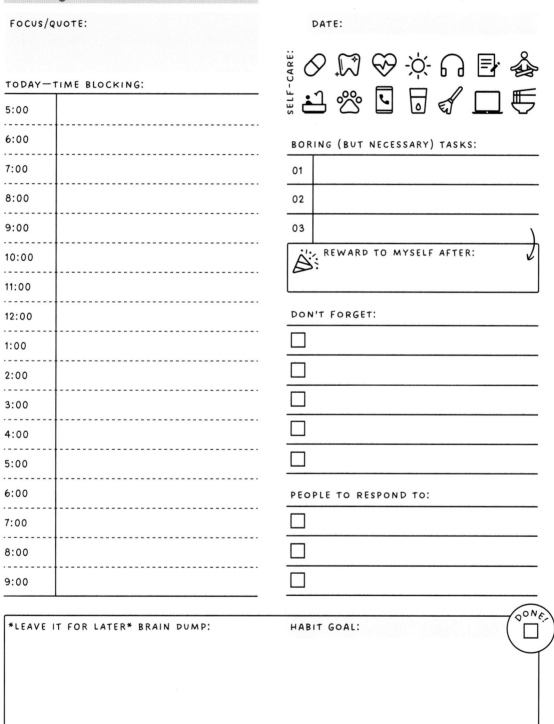

TODAY—TIME BLOCKING:

5:00	
6:00	
7:00	
8:00	
9:00	
10:00	
11:00	
12:00	
1:00	
2:00	
3:00	
4:00	
5:00	
6:00	
7:00	
8:00	
9:00	

BORING (BUT NECESSARY) TASKS:

01

02

03

REWARD TO MYSELF AFTER:

DON'T FORGET:

☐
☐
☐
☐
☐

PEOPLE TO RESPOND TO:

☐
☐
☐

LEAVE IT FOR LATER BRAIN DUMP:

HABIT GOAL:

DONE! ☐

Take 10, *Every 10* | REFLECT

Time to check in with yourself. You don't have to fill in everything—just the parts that speak to you.

HOW I'M FEELING:

DATE: / / SUN MON TUE WED THU FRI SAT ○○○○○○○

WINS (BIG OR SMALL):
- ☐
- ☐
- ☐

GLIMMERS:
- ☐
- ☐
- ☐

TRIGGERS:
- ☐
- ☐
- ☐

HOW I CELEBRATED:

FAVE PLAYLIST RIGHT NOW:

CURRENT HYPERFIXATION:

SELF-CARE WHEEL:

SCREEN-FREE TIME
SLEEP & REST
DENTAL HEALTH
EXERCISE
HEALTHY RELATIONSHIPS
NUTRITION
PLAY & CURIOSITY
MINDFULNESS

1 2 3 4 5 6 7 8 9 10

✳ Assess your self-care by coloring the wheel.
1 is lowest care, 10 is highest care.

HABIT CHECK-IN:

✳ Which habits did I do well or consistently?

✳ Which habits did I drop the ball on + why (e.g., not enough support/accountability)?

✳ <u>Why</u> are these habits important to me and my values?

✳ How will I feel if I integrate them?

Take 10, *Every 10* | RESET

Okay, now take the notes you need from the previous pages to move forward, at your own pace.

HABITS I'M WORKING ON:

TASKS I'M CARRYING FORWARD:
- ☐
- ☐
- ☐

TOP PRIORITIES:
- ☐
- ☐
- ☐

TOO-HARD BASKET:
- ☐
- ☐
- ☐

ON MY MIND:

＊ Use this space to journal, or write down things that are worrying you.

SOUL GOAL:

＊ See page 96 on Soul Goals.

QUICK COLOR TO CALM:

Color in only shades of <u>red</u>.

＊ Tip: Coloring in shades of the **same color** helps shift from divergent to convergent thinking.

PEP TALK/MANTRA MOVING FORWARD:

Daily focus friend

FOCUS/QUOTE:

DATE:

SELF-CARE:

TODAY—TIME BLOCKING:

5:00	
6:00	
7:00	
8:00	
9:00	
10:00	
11:00	
12:00	
1:00	
2:00	
3:00	
4:00	
5:00	
6:00	
7:00	
8:00	
9:00	

BORING (BUT NECESSARY) TASKS:

01

02

03

REWARD TO MYSELF AFTER:

DON'T FORGET:

☐

☐

☐

☐

☐

PEOPLE TO RESPOND TO:

☐

☐

☐

LEAVE IT FOR LATER BRAIN DUMP:

HABIT GOAL:

DONE!
☐

Daily focus friend

SUN MON TUE WED THU FRI SAT
○   ○   ○   ○   ○   ○   ○

FOCUS/QUOTE:

DATE:

SELF-CARE:

BORING (BUT NECESSARY) TASKS:

01	
02	
03	

REWARD TO MYSELF AFTER:

TODAY—TIME BLOCKING:

5:00	
6:00	
7:00	
8:00	
9:00	
10:00	
11:00	
12:00	
1:00	
2:00	
3:00	
4:00	
5:00	
6:00	
7:00	
8:00	
9:00	

DON'T FORGET:

☐
☐
☐
☐
☐

PEOPLE TO RESPOND TO:

☐
☐
☐

LEAVE IT FOR LATER BRAIN DUMP:

HABIT GOAL:

DONE! ☐

Daily focus friend

FOCUS/QUOTE:

DATE:

SELF-CARE:

TODAY—TIME BLOCKING:

5:00

6:00

7:00

8:00

9:00

10:00

11:00

12:00

1:00

2:00

3:00

4:00

5:00

6:00

7:00

8:00

9:00

BORING (BUT NECESSARY) TASKS:

01

02

03

🎉 REWARD TO MYSELF AFTER:

DON'T FORGET:

☐

☐

☐

☐

☐

PEOPLE TO RESPOND TO:

☐

☐

☐

LEAVE IT FOR LATER BRAIN DUMP:

HABIT GOAL:

DONE!
☐

Daily focus friend

FOCUS/QUOTE:

DATE:

SELF-CARE:

BORING (BUT NECESSARY) TASKS:

TODAY—TIME BLOCKING:

| 5:00 |
| 6:00 |
| 7:00 |
| 8:00 |
| 9:00 |
| 10:00 |
| 11:00 |
| 12:00 |
| 1:00 |
| 2:00 |
| 3:00 |
| 4:00 |
| 5:00 |
| 6:00 |
| 7:00 |
| 8:00 |
| 9:00 |

| 01 |
| 02 |
| 03 |

REWARD TO MYSELF AFTER:

DON'T FORGET:

☐

☐

☐

☐

☐

PEOPLE TO RESPOND TO:

☐

☐

☐

LEAVE IT FOR LATER BRAIN DUMP:

HABIT GOAL:

DONE!
☐

Daily focus friend

SUN MON TUE WED THU FRI SAT
○   ○   ○   ○   ○   ○   ○

FOCUS/QUOTE:

DATE:

SELF-CARE:

TODAY—TIME BLOCKING:

5:00	
6:00	
7:00	
8:00	
9:00	
10:00	
11:00	
12:00	
1:00	
2:00	
3:00	
4:00	
5:00	
6:00	
7:00	
8:00	
9:00	

BORING (BUT NECESSARY) TASKS:

01

02

03

REWARD TO MYSELF AFTER:

DON'T FORGET:

☐

☐

☐

☐

☐

PEOPLE TO RESPOND TO:

☐

☐

☐

LEAVE IT FOR LATER BRAIN DUMP:

HABIT GOAL:

DONE!
☐

Daily focus friend

FOCUS/QUOTE:

DATE:

SELF-CARE:

TODAY—TIME BLOCKING:

5:00	
6:00	
7:00	
8:00	
9:00	
10:00	
11:00	
12:00	
1:00	
2:00	
3:00	
4:00	
5:00	
6:00	
7:00	
8:00	
9:00	

BORING (BUT NECESSARY) TASKS:

01

02

03

🎉 REWARD TO MYSELF AFTER:

DON'T FORGET:

☐

☐

☐

☐

☐

PEOPLE TO RESPOND TO:

☐

☐

☐

LEAVE IT FOR LATER BRAIN DUMP:

HABIT GOAL:

DONE!
☐

Daily focus friend

SUN MON TUE WED THU FRI SAT
○   ○   ○   ○   ○   ○   ○

FOCUS/QUOTE:

DATE:

SELF-CARE:

TODAY—TIME BLOCKING:

5:00	
6:00	
7:00	
8:00	
9:00	
10:00	
11:00	
12:00	
1:00	
2:00	
3:00	
4:00	
5:00	
6:00	
7:00	
8:00	
9:00	

BORING (BUT NECESSARY) TASKS:

01

02

03

REWARD TO MYSELF AFTER:

DON'T FORGET:

☐

☐

☐

☐

☐

PEOPLE TO RESPOND TO:

☐

☐

☐

LEAVE IT FOR LATER BRAIN DUMP:

HABIT GOAL:

DONE!
☐

146

Daily focus friend

FOCUS/QUOTE:

DATE:

SELF-CARE:

TODAY—TIME BLOCKING:

5:00	
6:00	
7:00	
8:00	
9:00	
10:00	
11:00	
12:00	
1:00	
2:00	
3:00	
4:00	
5:00	
6:00	
7:00	
8:00	
9:00	

BORING (BUT NECESSARY) TASKS:

01

02

03

REWARD TO MYSELF AFTER:

DON'T FORGET:

☐
☐
☐
☐
☐

PEOPLE TO RESPOND TO:

☐
☐
☐

LEAVE IT FOR LATER BRAIN DUMP:

HABIT GOAL:

DONE!
☐

Daily focus friend

FOCUS/QUOTE:

DATE:

SELF-CARE:

TODAY—TIME BLOCKING:

5:00	
6:00	
7:00	
8:00	
9:00	
10:00	
11:00	
12:00	
1:00	
2:00	
3:00	
4:00	
5:00	
6:00	
7:00	
8:00	
9:00	

BORING (BUT NECESSARY) TASKS:

01

02

03

REWARD TO MYSELF AFTER:

DON'T FORGET:

☐
☐
☐
☐
☐

PEOPLE TO RESPOND TO:

☐
☐
☐

LEAVE IT FOR LATER BRAIN DUMP:

HABIT GOAL:

DONE!
☐

Daily focus friend

FOCUS/QUOTE:

DATE:

SELF-CARE:

TODAY—TIME BLOCKING:

5:00	
6:00	
7:00	
8:00	
9:00	
10:00	
11:00	
12:00	
1:00	
2:00	
3:00	
4:00	
5:00	
6:00	
7:00	
8:00	
9:00	

BORING (BUT NECESSARY) TASKS:

01

02

03

REWARD TO MYSELF AFTER:

DON'T FORGET:

☐

☐

☐

☐

☐

PEOPLE TO RESPOND TO:

☐

☐

☐

LEAVE IT FOR LATER BRAIN DUMP:

HABIT GOAL:

DONE!
☐

Take 10, *Every 10* | REFLECT

Time to check in with yourself. You don't have to fill in everything—just the parts that speak to you.

HOW I'M FEELING:

DATE: / /   MON TUE WED THU FRI SAT SUN
○ ○ ○ ○ ○ ○ ○

WINS (BIG OR SMALL):
☐
☐
☐

GLIMMERS: ✦ ✦
☐
☐
☐

TRIGGERS:
☐
☐
☐

HOW I CELEBRATED:

FAVE PLAYLIST RIGHT NOW:

CURRENT HYPERFIXATION:

SELF-CARE WHEEL:

SCREEN-FREE TIME · SLEEP & REST · DENTAL HEALTH · EXERCISE · HEALTHY RELATIONSHIPS · NUTRITION · PLAY & CURIOSITY · MINDFULNESS

1 2 3 4 5 6 7 8 9 10

✳ Assess your self-care by coloring the wheel.
1 is lowest care, 10 is highest care.

HABIT CHECK-IN:

✳ Which habits did I do well or consistently?

✳ Which habits did I drop the ball on + why (e.g., not enough support/accountability)?

✳ <u>Why</u> are these habits important to me and my values?

✳ How will I feel if I integrate them?

Take 10, *Every 10* | **RESET**

Okay, now take the notes you need from the previous pages to move forward, at your own pace.

HABITS I'M WORKING ON:

TASKS I'M CARRYING FORWARD:

☐

☐

☐

TOP PRIORITIES:

☐

☐

☐

TOO-HARD BASKET:

☐

☐

☐

ON MY MIND:

✳ *Use this space to journal, or write down things that are worrying you.*

SOUL GOAL:

✳ *See page 96 on Soul Goals.*

QUICK COLOR TO CALM:

Color in only shades of <u>orange</u>.

✳ *Tip: Coloring in shades of the **same color** helps shift from divergent to convergent thinking.*

PEP TALK/MANTRA MOVING FORWARD:

Daily focus friend

FOCUS/QUOTE:

DATE:

SELF-CARE:

TODAY—TIME BLOCKING:

| 5:00 |
| 6:00 |
| 7:00 |
| 8:00 |
| 9:00 |
| 10:00 |
| 11:00 |
| 12:00 |
| 1:00 |
| 2:00 |
| 3:00 |
| 4:00 |
| 5:00 |
| 6:00 |
| 7:00 |
| 8:00 |
| 9:00 |

BORING (BUT NECESSARY) TASKS:

01

02

03

REWARD TO MYSELF AFTER:

DON'T FORGET:

☐

☐

☐

☐

☐

PEOPLE TO RESPOND TO:

☐

☐

☐

LEAVE IT FOR LATER BRAIN DUMP:

HABIT GOAL:

DONE!
☐

Daily focus friend

FOCUS/QUOTE:

DATE:

SELF-CARE:

TODAY—TIME BLOCKING:

5:00

6:00

7:00

8:00

9:00

10:00

11:00

12:00

1:00

2:00

3:00

4:00

5:00

6:00

7:00

8:00

9:00

BORING (BUT NECESSARY) TASKS:

01

02

03

REWARD TO MYSELF AFTER:

DON'T FORGET:

☐
☐
☐
☐
☐

PEOPLE TO RESPOND TO:

☐
☐
☐

LEAVE IT FOR LATER BRAIN DUMP:

HABIT GOAL:

DONE!
☐

Daily focus friend

SUN MON TUE WED THU FRI SAT
◯   ◯   ◯   ◯   ◯   ◯   ◯

FOCUS/QUOTE:

DATE:

SELF-CARE:

TODAY—TIME BLOCKING:

5:00	
6:00	
7:00	
8:00	
9:00	
10:00	
11:00	
12:00	
1:00	
2:00	
3:00	
4:00	
5:00	
6:00	
7:00	
8:00	
9:00	

BORING (BUT NECESSARY) TASKS:

01

02

03

REWARD TO MYSELF AFTER:

DON'T FORGET:

- ☐
- ☐
- ☐
- ☐
- ☐

PEOPLE TO RESPOND TO:

- ☐
- ☐
- ☐

LEAVE IT FOR LATER BRAIN DUMP:

HABIT GOAL:

DONE! ☐

Daily focus friend

FOCUS/QUOTE:

DATE:

SELF-CARE:

BORING (BUT NECESSARY) TASKS:

TODAY—TIME BLOCKING:

5:00	
6:00	
7:00	
8:00	
9:00	
10:00	
11:00	
12:00	
1:00	
2:00	
3:00	
4:00	
5:00	
6:00	
7:00	
8:00	
9:00	

01

02

03

REWARD TO MYSELF AFTER:

DON'T FORGET:

☐
☐
☐
☐
☐

PEOPLE TO RESPOND TO:

☐
☐
☐

LEAVE IT FOR LATER BRAIN DUMP:

HABIT GOAL:

DONE!
☐

Daily focus friend

FOCUS/QUOTE:

DATE:

SELF-CARE:

TODAY—TIME BLOCKING:

5:00	
6:00	
7:00	
8:00	
9:00	
10:00	
11:00	
12:00	
1:00	
2:00	
3:00	
4:00	
5:00	
6:00	
7:00	
8:00	
9:00	

BORING (BUT NECESSARY) TASKS:

01

02

03

REWARD TO MYSELF AFTER:

DON'T FORGET:

☐
☐
☐
☐
☐

PEOPLE TO RESPOND TO:

☐
☐
☐

LEAVE IT FOR LATER BRAIN DUMP:

HABIT GOAL:

DONE!
☐

Daily focus friend

FOCUS/QUOTE:

DATE:

SELF-CARE:

TODAY—TIME BLOCKING:

5:00	
6:00	
7:00	
8:00	
9:00	
10:00	
11:00	
12:00	
1:00	
2:00	
3:00	
4:00	
5:00	
6:00	
7:00	
8:00	
9:00	

BORING (BUT NECESSARY) TASKS:

01
02
03

REWARD TO MYSELF AFTER:

DON'T FORGET:

☐
☐
☐
☐
☐

PEOPLE TO RESPOND TO:

☐
☐
☐

LEAVE IT FOR LATER BRAIN DUMP:

HABIT GOAL:

DONE!
☐

Daily focus friend

FOCUS/QUOTE:

DATE:

SELF-CARE:

TODAY—TIME BLOCKING:

5:00

6:00

7:00

8:00

9:00

10:00

11:00

12:00

1:00

2:00

3:00

4:00

5:00

6:00

7:00

8:00

9:00

BORING (BUT NECESSARY) TASKS:

01

02

03

REWARD TO MYSELF AFTER:

DON'T FORGET:

☐

☐

☐

☐

☐

PEOPLE TO RESPOND TO:

☐

☐

☐

LEAVE IT FOR LATER BRAIN DUMP:

HABIT GOAL:

DONE!
☐

Daily focus friend

FOCUS/QUOTE:

DATE:

SELF-CARE:

TODAY—TIME BLOCKING:

5:00	
6:00	
7:00	
8:00	
9:00	
10:00	
11:00	
12:00	
1:00	
2:00	
3:00	
4:00	
5:00	
6:00	
7:00	
8:00	
9:00	

BORING (BUT NECESSARY) TASKS:

01

02

03

REWARD TO MYSELF AFTER:

DON'T FORGET:

☐

☐

☐

☐

☐

PEOPLE TO RESPOND TO:

☐

☐

☐

LEAVE IT FOR LATER BRAIN DUMP:

HABIT GOAL:

DONE!
☐

Daily focus friend

FOCUS/QUOTE:

DATE:

SELF-CARE:

TODAY—TIME BLOCKING:

5:00

6:00

7:00

8:00

9:00

10:00

11:00

12:00

1:00

2:00

3:00

4:00

5:00

6:00

7:00

8:00

9:00

BORING (BUT NECESSARY) TASKS:

01

02

03

REWARD TO MYSELF AFTER:

DON'T FORGET:

☐

☐

☐

☐

☐

PEOPLE TO RESPOND TO:

☐

☐

☐

LEAVE IT FOR LATER BRAIN DUMP:

HABIT GOAL:

DONE!
☐

Daily focus friend

FOCUS/QUOTE:

DATE:

SELF-CARE:

TODAY—TIME BLOCKING:

5:00
6:00
7:00
8:00
9:00
10:00
11:00
12:00
1:00
2:00
3:00
4:00
5:00
6:00
7:00
8:00
9:00

BORING (BUT NECESSARY) TASKS:

01

02

03

REWARD TO MYSELF AFTER:

DON'T FORGET:

☐
☐
☐
☐
☐

PEOPLE TO RESPOND TO:

☐
☐
☐

LEAVE IT FOR LATER BRAIN DUMP:

HABIT GOAL:

DONE!
☐

Take 10, *Every 10* | REFLECT

Time to check in with yourself. You don't have to fill in everything—just the parts that speak to you.

HOW I'M FEELING:

DATE: / /

SUN MON TUE WED THU FRI SAT
○ ○ ○ ○ ○ ○ ○

WINS (BIG OR SMALL):
- ☐
- ☐
- ☐

GLIMMERS:
- ☐
- ☐
- ☐

TRIGGERS:
- ☐
- ☐
- ☐

HOW I CELEBRATED:

FAVE PLAYLIST RIGHT NOW:

CURRENT HYPERFIXATION:

SELF-CARE WHEEL:

SCREEN-FREE TIME · SLEEP & REST · DENTAL HEALTH · EXERCISE · HEALTHY RELATIONSHIPS · NUTRITION · PLAY & CURIOSITY · MINDFULNESS

1 2 3 4 5 6 7 8 9 10

✳ Assess your self-care by coloring the wheel.
1 is lowest care, 10 is highest care.

HABIT CHECK-IN:

✳ Which habits did I do well or consistently?

✳ Which habits did I drop the ball on + why (e.g., not enough support/accountability)?

✳ *Why* are these habits important to me and my values?

✳ How will I feel if I integrate them?

Take 10, *Every 10* | RESET

Okay, now take the notes you need from the previous pages to move forward, at your own pace.

HABITS I'M WORKING ON:

TASKS I'M CARRYING FORWARD:
- ☐
- ☐
- ☐

TOP PRIORITIES:
- ☐
- ☐
- ☐

TOO-HARD BASKET:
- ☐
- ☐
- ☐

ON MY MIND:

✳ *Use this space to journal, or write down things that are worrying you.*

SOUL GOAL:

✳ *See page 96 on Soul Goals.*

QUICK COLOR TO CALM:

Color in only shades of <u>blue</u>.

✳ *Tip: Coloring in shades of the **same color** helps shift from divergent to convergent thinking.*

PEP TALK/MANTRA MOVING FORWARD:

Daily focus friend

FOCUS/QUOTE:

DATE:

SELF-CARE:

TODAY—TIME BLOCKING:

5:00

6:00

7:00

8:00

9:00

10:00

11:00

12:00

1:00

2:00

3:00

4:00

5:00

6:00

7:00

8:00

9:00

BORING (BUT NECESSARY) TASKS:

01

02

03

🎉 REWARD TO MYSELF AFTER:

DON'T FORGET:

☐

☐

☐

☐

☐

PEOPLE TO RESPOND TO:

☐

☐

☐

LEAVE IT FOR LATER BRAIN DUMP:

HABIT GOAL:

DONE!
☐

Daily focus friend

FOCUS/QUOTE:

DATE:

SELF-CARE:

TODAY—TIME BLOCKING:

5:00
6:00
7:00
8:00
9:00
10:00
11:00
12:00
1:00
2:00
3:00
4:00
5:00
6:00
7:00
8:00
9:00

BORING (BUT NECESSARY) TASKS:

01

02

03

REWARD TO MYSELF AFTER:

DON'T FORGET:

☐

☐

☐

☐

☐

PEOPLE TO RESPOND TO:

☐

☐

☐

LEAVE IT FOR LATER BRAIN DUMP:

HABIT GOAL:

DONE!
☐

Daily focus friend

FOCUS/QUOTE:

DATE:

TODAY—TIME BLOCKING:

5:00	
6:00	
7:00	
8:00	
9:00	
10:00	
11:00	
12:00	
1:00	
2:00	
3:00	
4:00	
5:00	
6:00	
7:00	
8:00	
9:00	

SELF-CARE:

BORING (BUT NECESSARY) TASKS:

01

02

03

🎉 REWARD TO MYSELF AFTER:

DON'T FORGET:

☐
☐
☐
☐
☐

PEOPLE TO RESPOND TO:

☐
☐
☐

LEAVE IT FOR LATER BRAIN DUMP:

HABIT GOAL:

DONE! ☐

Daily focus friend

FOCUS/QUOTE:

DATE:

SELF-CARE:

TODAY—TIME BLOCKING:

| 5:00 |
| 6:00 |
| 7:00 |
| 8:00 |
| 9:00 |
| 10:00 |
| 11:00 |
| 12:00 |
| 1:00 |
| 2:00 |
| 3:00 |
| 4:00 |
| 5:00 |
| 6:00 |
| 7:00 |
| 8:00 |
| 9:00 |

BORING (BUT NECESSARY) TASKS:

01

02

03

🎉 REWARD TO MYSELF AFTER:

DON'T FORGET:

☐
☐
☐
☐
☐

PEOPLE TO RESPOND TO:

☐
☐
☐

LEAVE IT FOR LATER BRAIN DUMP:

HABIT GOAL:

DONE! ☐

Daily focus friend

FOCUS/QUOTE:

DATE:

SELF-CARE:

TODAY—TIME BLOCKING:

5:00	
6:00	
7:00	
8:00	
9:00	
10:00	
11:00	
12:00	
1:00	
2:00	
3:00	
4:00	
5:00	
6:00	
7:00	
8:00	
9:00	

BORING (BUT NECESSARY) TASKS:

01

02

03

REWARD TO MYSELF AFTER:

DON'T FORGET:

☐
☐
☐
☐
☐

PEOPLE TO RESPOND TO:

☐
☐
☐

LEAVE IT FOR LATER BRAIN DUMP:

HABIT GOAL:

DONE! ☐

Daily focus friend

FOCUS/QUOTE:

DATE:

SELF-CARE:

TODAY—TIME BLOCKING:

5:00	
6:00	
7:00	
8:00	
9:00	
10:00	
11:00	
12:00	
1:00	
2:00	
3:00	
4:00	
5:00	
6:00	
7:00	
8:00	
9:00	

BORING (BUT NECESSARY) TASKS:

01

02

03

REWARD TO MYSELF AFTER:

DON'T FORGET:

☐
☐
☐
☐
☐

PEOPLE TO RESPOND TO:

☐
☐
☐

LEAVE IT FOR LATER BRAIN DUMP:

HABIT GOAL:

DONE!
☐

Daily focus friend

FOCUS/QUOTE: DATE:

SELF-CARE:

TODAY—TIME BLOCKING:

5:00	
6:00	
7:00	
8:00	
9:00	
10:00	
11:00	
12:00	
1:00	
2:00	
3:00	
4:00	
5:00	
6:00	
7:00	
8:00	
9:00	

BORING (BUT NECESSARY) TASKS:

01

02

03

REWARD TO MYSELF AFTER:

DON'T FORGET:

☐
☐
☐
☐
☐

PEOPLE TO RESPOND TO:

☐
☐
☐

LEAVE IT FOR LATER BRAIN DUMP: HABIT GOAL:

DONE!
☐

Daily focus friend

SUN   MON   TUE   WED   THU   FRI   SAT
○   ○   ○   ○   ○   ○   ○

FOCUS/QUOTE:

DATE:

SELF-CARE:

TODAY—TIME BLOCKING:

5:00	
6:00	
7:00	
8:00	
9:00	
10:00	
11:00	
12:00	
1:00	
2:00	
3:00	
4:00	
5:00	
6:00	
7:00	
8:00	
9:00	

BORING (BUT NECESSARY) TASKS:

01

02

03

REWARD TO MYSELF AFTER:

DON'T FORGET:

☐
☐
☐
☐
☐

PEOPLE TO RESPOND TO:

☐
☐
☐

LEAVE IT FOR LATER BRAIN DUMP:

HABIT GOAL:

DONE!
☐

Daily focus friend

FOCUS/QUOTE:

DATE:

SELF-CARE:

TODAY—TIME BLOCKING:

5:00	
6:00	
7:00	
8:00	
9:00	
10:00	
11:00	
12:00	
1:00	
2:00	
3:00	
4:00	
5:00	
6:00	
7:00	
8:00	
9:00	

BORING (BUT NECESSARY) TASKS:

01

02

03

REWARD TO MYSELF AFTER:

DON'T FORGET:

☐

☐

☐

☐

☐

PEOPLE TO RESPOND TO:

☐

☐

☐

LEAVE IT FOR LATER BRAIN DUMP:

HABIT GOAL:

DONE!
☐

Daily focus friend

FOCUS/QUOTE:

DATE:

SELF-CARE:

TODAY—TIME BLOCKING:

| 5:00 |
| 6:00 |
| 7:00 |
| 8:00 |
| 9:00 |
| 10:00 |
| 11:00 |
| 12:00 |
| 1:00 |
| 2:00 |
| 3:00 |
| 4:00 |
| 5:00 |
| 6:00 |
| 7:00 |
| 8:00 |
| 9:00 |

BORING (BUT NECESSARY) TASKS:

01

02

03

REWARD TO MYSELF AFTER:

DON'T FORGET:

- [ ]
- [ ]
- [ ]
- [ ]
- [ ]

PEOPLE TO RESPOND TO:

- [ ]
- [ ]
- [ ]

LEAVE IT FOR LATER BRAIN DUMP:

HABIT GOAL:

DONE!
- [ ]

Take 10, *Every 10* | REFLECT

Time to check in with yourself. You don't have to fill in everything—just the parts that speak to you.

HOW I'M FEELING:

DATE: / /

SUN MON TUE WED THU FRI SAT
○ ○ ○ ○ ○ ○ ○

WINS (BIG OR SMALL):
- ☐
- ☐
- ☐

GLIMMERS:
- ☐
- ☐
- ☐

TRIGGERS:
- ☐
- ☐

HOW I CELEBRATED:

FAVE PLAYLIST RIGHT NOW:

CURRENT HYPERFIXATION:

SELF-CARE WHEEL:

SCREEN-FREE TIME
SLEEP & REST
MINDFULNESS
DENTAL HEALTH
PLAY & CURIOSITY
EXERCISE
NUTRITION
HEALTHY RELATIONSHIPS

1 2 3 4 5 6 7 8 9 10

✳ Assess your self-care by coloring the wheel.
1 is lowest care, 10 is highest care.

HABIT CHECK-IN:

✳ Which habits did I do well or consistently?

✳ Which habits did I drop the ball on + why (e.g., not enough support/accountability)?

✳ Why are these habits important to me and my values?

✳ How will I feel if I integrate them?

Take 10, *Every 10* | **RESET**

Okay, now take the notes you need from the previous pages to move forward, at your own pace.

HABITS I'M WORKING ON:

TASKS I'M CARRYING FORWARD:

- [ ]
- [ ]
- [ ]

TOP PRIORITIES:

- [ ]
- [ ]
- [ ]

TOO-HARD BASKET:

- [ ]
- [ ]
- [ ]

ON MY MIND:

✳ Use this space to journal, or write down things that are worrying you.

SOUL GOAL:

✳ See page 96 on Soul Goals.

QUICK COLOR TO CALM:

Color in only shades of <u>pink</u>.

✳ Tip: Coloring in shades of the **same color** helps shift from divergent to convergent thinking.

PEP TALK/MANTRA MOVING FORWARD:

Daily focus friend

FOCUS/QUOTE:

DATE:

SELF-CARE:

TODAY—TIME BLOCKING:

5:00	
6:00	
7:00	
8:00	
9:00	
10:00	
11:00	
12:00	
1:00	
2:00	
3:00	
4:00	
5:00	
6:00	
7:00	
8:00	
9:00	

BORING (BUT NECESSARY) TASKS:

01

02

03

🎉 REWARD TO MYSELF AFTER:

DON'T FORGET:

☐
☐
☐
☐
☐

PEOPLE TO RESPOND TO:

☐
☐
☐

LEAVE IT FOR LATER BRAIN DUMP:

HABIT GOAL:

DONE! ☐

Daily focus friend

FOCUS/QUOTE:

DATE:

SELF-CARE:

TODAY—TIME BLOCKING:

5:00	
6:00	
7:00	
8:00	
9:00	
10:00	
11:00	
12:00	
1:00	
2:00	
3:00	
4:00	
5:00	
6:00	
7:00	
8:00	
9:00	

BORING (BUT NECESSARY) TASKS:

01	
02	
03	

REWARD TO MYSELF AFTER:

DON'T FORGET:

- ☐
- ☐
- ☐
- ☐
- ☐

PEOPLE TO RESPOND TO:

- ☐
- ☐
- ☐

LEAVE IT FOR LATER BRAIN DUMP:

HABIT GOAL:

DONE! ☐

Daily focus friend

FOCUS/QUOTE:

DATE:

SELF-CARE:

TODAY—TIME BLOCKING:

5:00	
6:00	
7:00	
8:00	
9:00	
10:00	
11:00	
12:00	
1:00	
2:00	
3:00	
4:00	
5:00	
6:00	
7:00	
8:00	
9:00	

BORING (BUT NECESSARY) TASKS:

01

02

03

REWARD TO MYSELF AFTER:

DON'T FORGET:

☐
☐
☐
☐
☐

PEOPLE TO RESPOND TO:

☐
☐
☐

LEAVE IT FOR LATER BRAIN DUMP:

HABIT GOAL:

DONE!
☐

Daily focus friend

SUN MON TUE WED THU FRI SAT
○   ○   ○   ○   ○   ○   ○

FOCUS/QUOTE:

DATE:

SELF-CARE:

TODAY—TIME BLOCKING:

5:00	
6:00	
7:00	
8:00	
9:00	
10:00	
11:00	
12:00	
1:00	
2:00	
3:00	
4:00	
5:00	
6:00	
7:00	
8:00	
9:00	

BORING (BUT NECESSARY) TASKS:

01

02

03

REWARD TO MYSELF AFTER:

DON'T FORGET:

☐
☐
☐
☐
☐

PEOPLE TO RESPOND TO:

☐
☐
☐

LEAVE IT FOR LATER BRAIN DUMP:

HABIT GOAL:

DONE!
☐

Daily focus friend

FOCUS/QUOTE:

DATE:

SELF-CARE:

TODAY—TIME BLOCKING:

5:00	
6:00	
7:00	
8:00	
9:00	
10:00	
11:00	
12:00	
1:00	
2:00	
3:00	
4:00	
5:00	
6:00	
7:00	
8:00	
9:00	

BORING (BUT NECESSARY) TASKS:

01

02

03

REWARD TO MYSELF AFTER:

DON'T FORGET:

☐
☐
☐
☐
☐

PEOPLE TO RESPOND TO:

☐
☐
☐

LEAVE IT FOR LATER BRAIN DUMP:

HABIT GOAL:

DONE! ☐

Daily focus friend

SUN   MON   TUE   WED   THU   FRI   SAT
○   ○   ○   ○   ○   ○   ○

FOCUS/QUOTE:

DATE:

SELF-CARE:

TODAY—TIME BLOCKING:

5:00

6:00

7:00

8:00

9:00

10:00

11:00

12:00

1:00

2:00

3:00

4:00

5:00

6:00

7:00

8:00

9:00

BORING (BUT NECESSARY) TASKS:

01

02

03

REWARD TO MYSELF AFTER:

DON'T FORGET:

☐

☐

☐

☐

☐

PEOPLE TO RESPOND TO:

☐

☐

☐

LEAVE IT FOR LATER BRAIN DUMP:

HABIT GOAL:

DONE!
☐

Daily focus friend

SUN MON TUE WED THU FRI SAT
○   ○   ○   ○   ○   ○   ○

FOCUS/QUOTE:

DATE:

SELF-CARE:

TODAY—TIME BLOCKING:

5:00

6:00

7:00

8:00

9:00

10:00

11:00

12:00

1:00

2:00

3:00

4:00

5:00

6:00

7:00

8:00

9:00

BORING (BUT NECESSARY) TASKS:

01

02

03

🎉 REWARD TO MYSELF AFTER:

DON'T FORGET:

☐

☐

☐

☐

☐

PEOPLE TO RESPOND TO:

☐

☐

☐

LEAVE IT FOR LATER BRAIN DUMP:

HABIT GOAL:

DONE!
☐

Daily focus friend

FOCUS/QUOTE:

DATE:

SELF-CARE:

TODAY—TIME BLOCKING:

5:00

6:00

7:00

8:00

9:00

10:00

11:00

12:00

1:00

2:00

3:00

4:00

5:00

6:00

7:00

8:00

9:00

BORING (BUT NECESSARY) TASKS:

01

02

03

🎉 REWARD TO MYSELF AFTER:

DON'T FORGET:

☐

☐

☐

☐

☐

PEOPLE TO RESPOND TO:

☐

☐

☐

LEAVE IT FOR LATER BRAIN DUMP:

HABIT GOAL:

DONE!
☐

Daily focus friend

SUN MON TUE WED THU FRI SAT
○   ○   ○   ○   ○   ○   ○

FOCUS/QUOTE: DATE:

SELF-CARE:

TODAY—TIME BLOCKING:

5:00	
6:00	
7:00	
8:00	
9:00	
10:00	
11:00	
12:00	
1:00	
2:00	
3:00	
4:00	
5:00	
6:00	
7:00	
8:00	
9:00	

BORING (BUT NECESSARY) TASKS:

01

02

03

REWARD TO MYSELF AFTER:

DON'T FORGET:

☐
☐
☐
☐
☐

PEOPLE TO RESPOND TO:

☐
☐
☐

LEAVE IT FOR LATER BRAIN DUMP:

HABIT GOAL:

DONE!
☐

Daily focus friend

FOCUS/QUOTE:

DATE:

SELF-CARE:

TODAY—TIME BLOCKING:

5:00	
6:00	
7:00	
8:00	
9:00	
10:00	
11:00	
12:00	
1:00	
2:00	
3:00	
4:00	
5:00	
6:00	
7:00	
8:00	
9:00	

BORING (BUT NECESSARY) TASKS:

01

02

03

REWARD TO MYSELF AFTER:

DON'T FORGET:

☐
☐
☐
☐
☐

PEOPLE TO RESPOND TO:

☐
☐
☐

LEAVE IT FOR LATER BRAIN DUMP:

HABIT GOAL:

DONE!
☐

Take 10, *Every 10* | REFLECT

Time to check in with yourself. You don't have to fill in everything—just the parts that speak to you.

HOW I'M FEELING:

DATE: / /

SUN MON TUE WED THU FRI SAT
○ ○ ○ ○ ○ ○ ○

WINS (BIG OR SMALL):

☐

☐

☐

GLIMMERS:

☐

☐

☐

TRIGGERS:

☐

☐

☐

HOW I CELEBRATED:

FAVE PLAYLIST RIGHT NOW:

CURRENT HYPERFIXATION:

SELF-CARE WHEEL:

SCREEN-FREE TIME
SLEEP & REST
DENTAL HEALTH
EXERCISE
HEALTHY RELATIONSHIPS
NUTRITION
PLAY & CURIOSITY
MINDFULNESS

1 2 3 4 5 6 7 8 9 10

✳ Assess your self-care by coloring the wheel.
1 is lowest care, 10 is highest care.

HABIT CHECK-IN:

✳ Which habits did I do well or consistently?

✳ Which habits did I drop the ball on + why (e.g., not enough support/accountability)?

✳ <u>Why</u> are these habits important to me and my values?

✳ How will I feel if I integrate them?

Take 10, *Every 10* | RESET

Okay, now take the notes you need from the previous pages to move forward, at your own pace.

HABITS I'M WORKING ON:

TASKS I'M CARRYING FORWARD:
- ☐
- ☐
- ☐

TOP PRIORITIES:
- ☐
- ☐
- ☐

TOO-HARD BASKET:
- ☐
- ☐
- ☐

ON MY MIND:

✳ *Use this space to journal, or write down things that are worrying you.*

SOUL GOAL:

✳ *See page 96 on Soul Goals.*

QUICK COLOR TO CALM:

Color in only shades of green.

✳ *Tip: Coloring in shades of the **same color** helps shift from divergent to convergent thinking.*

PEP TALK/MANTRA MOVING FORWARD:

Daily focus friend

FOCUS/QUOTE:

DATE:

SELF-CARE:

TODAY—TIME BLOCKING:

5:00	
6:00	
7:00	
8:00	
9:00	
10:00	
11:00	
12:00	
1:00	
2:00	
3:00	
4:00	
5:00	
6:00	
7:00	
8:00	
9:00	

BORING (BUT NECESSARY) TASKS:

01

02

03

REWARD TO MYSELF AFTER:

DON'T FORGET:

☐

☐

☐

☐

☐

PEOPLE TO RESPOND TO:

☐

☐

☐

LEAVE IT FOR LATER BRAIN DUMP:

HABIT GOAL:

DONE! ☐

Daily focus friend

FOCUS/QUOTE:

DATE:

SELF-CARE:

TODAY—TIME BLOCKING:

5:00

6:00

7:00

8:00

9:00

10:00

11:00

12:00

1:00

2:00

3:00

4:00

5:00

6:00

7:00

8:00

9:00

BORING (BUT NECESSARY) TASKS:

01

02

03

🎉 REWARD TO MYSELF AFTER:

DON'T FORGET:

☐

☐

☐

☐

☐

PEOPLE TO RESPOND TO:

☐

☐

☐

LEAVE IT FOR LATER BRAIN DUMP:

HABIT GOAL:

DONE!
☐

Daily focus friend

SUN MON TUE WED THU FRI SAT
○   ○   ○   ○   ○   ○   ○

FOCUS/QUOTE:

DATE:

SELF-CARE:

TODAY—TIME BLOCKING:

5:00	
6:00	
7:00	
8:00	
9:00	
10:00	
11:00	
12:00	
1:00	
2:00	
3:00	
4:00	
5:00	
6:00	
7:00	
8:00	
9:00	

BORING (BUT NECESSARY) TASKS:

01

02

03

REWARD TO MYSELF AFTER:

DON'T FORGET:

☐
☐
☐
☐
☐

PEOPLE TO RESPOND TO:

☐
☐
☐

LEAVE IT FOR LATER BRAIN DUMP:

HABIT GOAL:

DONE! ☐

Daily focus friend

FOCUS/QUOTE:

DATE:

SELF-CARE:

TODAY—TIME BLOCKING:

5:00	
6:00	
7:00	
8:00	
9:00	
10:00	
11:00	
12:00	
1:00	
2:00	
3:00	
4:00	
5:00	
6:00	
7:00	
8:00	
9:00	

BORING (BUT NECESSARY) TASKS:

01

02

03

REWARD TO MYSELF AFTER:

DON'T FORGET:

☐
☐
☐
☐
☐

PEOPLE TO RESPOND TO:

☐
☐
☐

LEAVE IT FOR LATER BRAIN DUMP:

HABIT GOAL:

DONE!
☐

Daily focus friend

FOCUS/QUOTE:

DATE:

SELF-CARE:

TODAY—TIME BLOCKING:

5:00	
6:00	
7:00	
8:00	
9:00	
10:00	
11:00	
12:00	
1:00	
2:00	
3:00	
4:00	
5:00	
6:00	
7:00	
8:00	
9:00	

BORING (BUT NECESSARY) TASKS:

01

02

03

REWARD TO MYSELF AFTER:

DON'T FORGET:

☐
☐
☐
☐
☐

PEOPLE TO RESPOND TO:

☐
☐
☐

LEAVE IT FOR LATER BRAIN DUMP:

HABIT GOAL:

DONE! ☐

Daily focus friend

FOCUS/QUOTE:

DATE:

SELF-CARE:

TODAY—TIME BLOCKING:

5:00	
6:00	
7:00	
8:00	
9:00	
10:00	
11:00	
12:00	
1:00	
2:00	
3:00	
4:00	
5:00	
6:00	
7:00	
8:00	
9:00	

BORING (BUT NECESSARY) TASKS:

01

02

03

REWARD TO MYSELF AFTER:

DON'T FORGET:

☐

☐

☐

☐

☐

PEOPLE TO RESPOND TO:

☐

☐

☐

LEAVE IT FOR LATER BRAIN DUMP:

HABIT GOAL:

DONE!
☐

Daily focus friend

SUN MON TUE WED THU FRI SAT
○   ○   ○   ○   ○   ○   ○

FOCUS/QUOTE:

DATE:

SELF-CARE:

TODAY—TIME BLOCKING:

5:00	
6:00	
7:00	
8:00	
9:00	
10:00	
11:00	
12:00	
1:00	
2:00	
3:00	
4:00	
5:00	
6:00	
7:00	
8:00	
9:00	

BORING (BUT NECESSARY) TASKS:

01

02

03

REWARD TO MYSELF AFTER:

DON'T FORGET:

☐
☐
☐
☐
☐

PEOPLE TO RESPOND TO:

☐
☐
☐

LEAVE IT FOR LATER BRAIN DUMP:

HABIT GOAL:

DONE!
☐

Daily focus friend

○ ○ ○ ○ ○ ○ ○

FOCUS/QUOTE:

DATE:

SELF-CARE:

BORING (BUT NECESSARY) TASKS:

TODAY—TIME BLOCKING:

5:00	
6:00	
7:00	
8:00	
9:00	
10:00	
11:00	
12:00	
1:00	
2:00	
3:00	
4:00	
5:00	
6:00	
7:00	
8:00	
9:00	

01

02

03

REWARD TO MYSELF AFTER:

DON'T FORGET:

☐
☐
☐
☐
☐

PEOPLE TO RESPOND TO:

☐
☐
☐

LEAVE IT FOR LATER BRAIN DUMP:

HABIT GOAL:

DONE!
☐

Daily focus friend

FOCUS/QUOTE: DATE:

SELF-CARE:

TODAY—TIME BLOCKING:

5:00	
6:00	
7:00	
8:00	
9:00	
10:00	
11:00	
12:00	
1:00	
2:00	
3:00	
4:00	
5:00	
6:00	
7:00	
8:00	
9:00	

BORING (BUT NECESSARY) TASKS:

01

02

03

REWARD TO MYSELF AFTER:

DON'T FORGET:

☐
☐
☐
☐
☐

PEOPLE TO RESPOND TO:

☐
☐
☐

LEAVE IT FOR LATER BRAIN DUMP:

HABIT GOAL:

DONE!
☐

Daily focus friend

FOCUS/QUOTE:

DATE:

SELF-CARE:

TODAY—TIME BLOCKING:

5:00	
6:00	
7:00	
8:00	
9:00	
10:00	
11:00	
12:00	
1:00	
2:00	
3:00	
4:00	
5:00	
6:00	
7:00	
8:00	
9:00	

BORING (BUT NECESSARY) TASKS:

01

02

03

REWARD TO MYSELF AFTER:

DON'T FORGET:

☐
☐
☐
☐
☐

PEOPLE TO RESPOND TO:

☐
☐
☐

LEAVE IT FOR LATER BRAIN DUMP:

HABIT GOAL:

DONE! ☐

Take 10, *Every 10* | REFLECT

Time to check in with yourself. You don't have to fill in everything—just the parts that speak to you.

HOW I'M FEELING:

DATE: / /

SUN MON TUE WED THU FRI SAT
○ ○ ○ ○ ○ ○ ○

WINS (BIG OR SMALL):

☐

☐

☐

GLIMMERS:

☐

☐

☐

TRIGGERS:

☐

☐

☐

HOW I CELEBRATED:

FAVE PLAYLIST RIGHT NOW:

CURRENT HYPERFIXATION:

SELF-CARE WHEEL:

SCREEN-FREE TIME

SLEEP & REST

MINDFULNESS

DENTAL HEALTH

PLAY & CURIOSITY

EXERCISE

NUTRITION

HEALTHY RELATIONSHIPS

1 2 3 4 5 6 7 8 9 10

✳ Assess your self-care by coloring the wheel.
1 is lowest care, 10 is highest care.

HABIT CHECK-IN:

✳ Which habits did I do well or consistently?

✳ Which habits did I drop the ball on + why (e.g., not enough support/accountability)?

✳ <u>Why</u> are these habits important to me and my values?

✳ How will I feel if I integrate them?

Take 10, *Every 10* | RESET

Okay, now take the notes you need from the previous pages to move forward, at your own pace.

HABITS I'M WORKING ON:

TASKS I'M CARRYING FORWARD:
- [ ]
- [ ]
- [ ]

TOP PRIORITIES:
- [ ]
- [ ]
- [ ]

TOO-HARD BASKET:
- [ ]
- [ ]
- [ ]

ON MY MIND:

✳ Use this space to journal, or write down things that are worrying you.

SOUL GOAL:

✳ See page 96 on Soul Goals.

QUICK COLOR TO CALM:

Color in only shades of <u>purple</u>.

✳ Tip: Coloring in shades of the **same color** helps shift from divergent to convergent thinking.

PEP TALK/MANTRA MOVING FORWARD:

Daily focus friend

SUN ○ MON ○ TUE ○ WED ○ THU ○ FRI ○ SAT ○

FOCUS/QUOTE:

DATE:

TODAY—TIME BLOCKING:

| 5:00 |
| 6:00 |
| 7:00 |
| 8:00 |
| 9:00 |
| 10:00 |
| 11:00 |
| 12:00 |
| 1:00 |
| 2:00 |
| 3:00 |
| 4:00 |
| 5:00 |
| 6:00 |
| 7:00 |
| 8:00 |
| 9:00 |

SELF-CARE:

BORING (BUT NECESSARY) TASKS:

01

02

03

🎉 REWARD TO MYSELF AFTER:

DON'T FORGET:

☐
☐
☐
☐
☐

PEOPLE TO RESPOND TO:

☐
☐
☐

LEAVE IT FOR LATER BRAIN DUMP:

HABIT GOAL:

DONE! ☐

200

Daily focus friend

FOCUS/QUOTE:

DATE:

SELF-CARE:

TODAY—TIME BLOCKING:

5:00	
6:00	
7:00	
8:00	
9:00	
10:00	
11:00	
12:00	
1:00	
2:00	
3:00	
4:00	
5:00	
6:00	
7:00	
8:00	
9:00	

BORING (BUT NECESSARY) TASKS:

01

02

03

REWARD TO MYSELF AFTER:

DON'T FORGET:

☐
☐
☐
☐
☐

PEOPLE TO RESPOND TO:

☐
☐
☐

LEAVE IT FOR LATER BRAIN DUMP:

HABIT GOAL:

DONE!
☐

Daily focus friend

SUN MON TUE WED THU FRI SAT
○   ○   ○   ○   ○   ○   ○

FOCUS/QUOTE:

DATE:

SELF-CARE:

TODAY—TIME BLOCKING:

5:00	
6:00	
7:00	
8:00	
9:00	
10:00	
11:00	
12:00	
1:00	
2:00	
3:00	
4:00	
5:00	
6:00	
7:00	
8:00	
9:00	

BORING (BUT NECESSARY) TASKS:

01

02

03

REWARD TO MYSELF AFTER:

DON'T FORGET:

☐

☐

☐

☐

☐

PEOPLE TO RESPOND TO:

☐

☐

☐

LEAVE IT FOR LATER BRAIN DUMP:

HABIT GOAL:

DONE!
☐

Daily focus friend

FOCUS/QUOTE:

DATE:

SELF-CARE:

TODAY—TIME BLOCKING:

5:00	
6:00	
7:00	
8:00	
9:00	
10:00	
11:00	
12:00	
1:00	
2:00	
3:00	
4:00	
5:00	
6:00	
7:00	
8:00	
9:00	

BORING (BUT NECESSARY) TASKS:

01
02
03

REWARD TO MYSELF AFTER:

DON'T FORGET:

☐
☐
☐
☐
☐

PEOPLE TO RESPOND TO:

☐
☐
☐

LEAVE IT FOR LATER BRAIN DUMP:

HABIT GOAL:

DONE! ☐

Daily focus friend

FOCUS/QUOTE:

DATE:

SELF-CARE:

TODAY—TIME BLOCKING:

5:00	
6:00	
7:00	
8:00	
9:00	
10:00	
11:00	
12:00	
1:00	
2:00	
3:00	
4:00	
5:00	
6:00	
7:00	
8:00	
9:00	

BORING (BUT NECESSARY) TASKS:

01

02

03

REWARD TO MYSELF AFTER:

DON'T FORGET:

☐
☐
☐
☐
☐

PEOPLE TO RESPOND TO:

☐
☐
☐

LEAVE IT FOR LATER BRAIN DUMP:

HABIT GOAL:

DONE! ☐

Daily focus friend

SUN   MON   TUE   WED   THU   FRI   SAT

○   ○   ○   ○   ○   ○   ○

FOCUS/QUOTE:

DATE:

SELF-CARE:

TODAY—TIME BLOCKING:

5:00

6:00

7:00

8:00

9:00

10:00

11:00

12:00

1:00

2:00

3:00

4:00

5:00

6:00

7:00

8:00

9:00

BORING (BUT NECESSARY) TASKS:

01

02

03

🎉 REWARD TO MYSELF AFTER:

DON'T FORGET:

☐

☐

☐

☐

☐

PEOPLE TO RESPOND TO:

☐

☐

☐

LEAVE IT FOR LATER BRAIN DUMP:

HABIT GOAL:

DONE! ☐

Daily focus friend

FOCUS/QUOTE:

DATE:

SELF-CARE:

TODAY—TIME BLOCKING:

5:00	
6:00	
7:00	
8:00	
9:00	
10:00	
11:00	
12:00	
1:00	
2:00	
3:00	
4:00	
5:00	
6:00	
7:00	
8:00	
9:00	

BORING (BUT NECESSARY) TASKS:

01

02

03

REWARD TO MYSELF AFTER:

DON'T FORGET:

☐

☐

☐

☐

☐

PEOPLE TO RESPOND TO:

☐

☐

☐

LEAVE IT FOR LATER BRAIN DUMP:

HABIT GOAL:

DONE!
☐

Daily focus friend

SUN MON TUE WED THU FRI SAT
○   ○   ○   ○   ○   ○   ○

FOCUS/QUOTE:

DATE:

SELF-CARE:

TODAY—TIME BLOCKING:

5:00	
6:00	
7:00	
8:00	
9:00	
10:00	
11:00	
12:00	
1:00	
2:00	
3:00	
4:00	
5:00	
6:00	
7:00	
8:00	
9:00	

BORING (BUT NECESSARY) TASKS:

01
02
03

REWARD TO MYSELF AFTER:

DON'T FORGET:

☐
☐
☐
☐
☐

PEOPLE TO RESPOND TO:

☐
☐
☐

LEAVE IT FOR LATER BRAIN DUMP:

HABIT GOAL:

DONE!
☐

Daily focus friend

○ ○ ○ ○ ○ ○ ○

FOCUS/QUOTE: _____

DATE: _____

SELF-CARE:

TODAY—TIME BLOCKING:

5:00	
6:00	
7:00	
8:00	
9:00	
10:00	
11:00	
12:00	
1:00	
2:00	
3:00	
4:00	
5:00	
6:00	
7:00	
8:00	
9:00	

BORING (BUT NECESSARY) TASKS:

01 _____
02 _____
03 _____

REWARD TO MYSELF AFTER:

DON'T FORGET:

☐ _____
☐ _____
☐ _____
☐ _____
☐ _____

PEOPLE TO RESPOND TO:

☐ _____
☐ _____
☐ _____

LEAVE IT FOR LATER BRAIN DUMP:

HABIT GOAL:

DONE! ☐

Daily focus friend

FOCUS/QUOTE:

DATE:

SELF-CARE:

TODAY—TIME BLOCKING:

5:00	
6:00	
7:00	
8:00	
9:00	
10:00	
11:00	
12:00	
1:00	
2:00	
3:00	
4:00	
5:00	
6:00	
7:00	
8:00	
9:00	

BORING (BUT NECESSARY) TASKS:

01

02

03

REWARD TO MYSELF AFTER:

DON'T FORGET:

☐

☐

☐

☐

☐

PEOPLE TO RESPOND TO:

☐

☐

☐

LEAVE IT FOR LATER BRAIN DUMP:

HABIT GOAL:

DONE!
☐

Take 10, *Every 10* | REFLECT

Time to check in with yourself. You don't have to fill in everything—just the parts that speak to you.

HOW I'M FEELING:

DATE: / /   SUN MON TUE WED THU FRI SAT
○ ○ ○ ○ ○ ○ ○

WINS (BIG OR SMALL):
☐
☐
☐

GLIMMERS:
☐
☐
☐

TRIGGERS:
☐
☐
☐

HOW I CELEBRATED:

FAVE PLAYLIST RIGHT NOW:

CURRENT HYPERFIXATION:

SELF-CARE WHEEL:

SCREEN-FREE TIME
SLEEP & REST
MINDFULNESS
DENTAL HEALTH
PLAY & CURIOSITY
EXERCISE
NUTRITION
HEALTHY RELATIONSHIPS

1 2 3 4 5 6 7 8 9 10

✳ Assess your self-care by coloring the wheel.
1 is lowest care, 10 is highest care.

HABIT CHECK-IN:

✳ Which habits did I do well or consistently?

✳ Which habits did I drop the ball on + why
(e.g., not enough support/accountability)?

✳ <u>Why</u> are these habits important to me and
my values?

✳ How will I feel if I integrate them?

Take 10, *Every 10* | RESET

Okay, now take the notes you need from the previous pages to move forward, at your own pace.

HABITS I'M WORKING ON:

TASKS I'M CARRYING FORWARD:
- ☐
- ☐
- ☐

TOP PRIORITIES:
- ☐
- ☐
- ☐

TOO-HARD BASKET:
- ☐
- ☐
- ☐

ON MY MIND:

＊ *Use this space to journal, or write down things that are worrying you.*

SOUL GOAL:

＊ *See page 96 on Soul Goals.*

QUICK COLOR TO CALM:

Color in only shades of <u>yellow</u>.

＊ *Tip: Coloring in shades of the **same color** helps shift from divergent to convergent thinking.*

PEP TALK/MANTRA MOVING FORWARD:

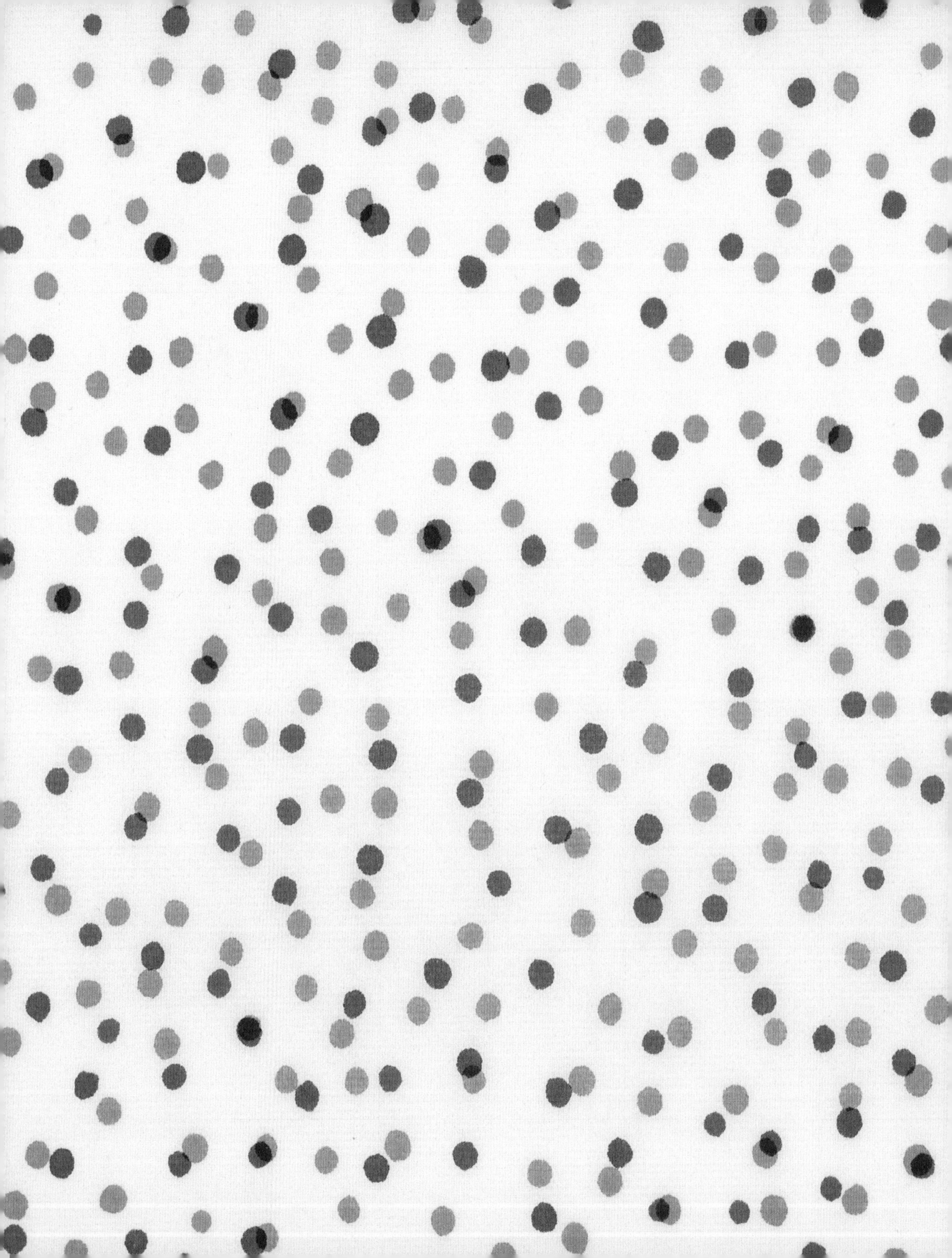

When you've used up the templates in the book, visit futureadhd.com/templates to download more.

The
Template
Toolbox

In this section you'll find a collection of ADHD-specific templates. Use these lists and organizational tools to take the tsunami of "popcorn" thoughts, life admin tasks, creative ideas, rabbit holes and divergent paths pinging away in your brain, and create some order.

#ADHDtax tracker

If you're unfamiliar, #ADHDtax references moments where you forget something (due to your ADHD brain), and as a result, you lose money or a valuable item. For example, while caught up in your own thoughts on the train, you leave your $300 earbuds behind on the train seat.

DESCRIBE THE ADHD TAX INCIDENT	STRATEGIES SO I DON'T DO THIS AGAIN

Cart: the 24-hour rule

Our ADHD brains looove a burst of impulsivity. One minute we're scrolling, the next minute we're five items deep in an online shopping cart and about to click "purchase" on $187. Write down those items here and see whether you still feel that burning desire to buy 24 hours later. Your bank account will thank you!

ONLINE STORE	ITEMS IN MY BASKET RIGHT NOW	⊗	⊘

Chill-out checklist

Because our ADHD brain can be a tad forgetful sometimes, we'll discover an awesome hack or relaxation technique that our brain loves, do it a million times in a week and then get so over it, we'll drop it and forget about it. Before this happens, note your current obsession—fave music playlists, apps, stretching/yoga exercises and go-to meditations—so you can find them again.

MEDITATIONS

STRETCHING/YOGA EXERCISES

APPS

MUSIC PLAYLISTS

Tip: Binaural beats have been shown
to be really effective for ADHD.

Books I started

We love to read 10 books at once, don't we? Note down your current reads here, so when you bounce to the next topic of interest, you can pop back to finish anytime.

BOOK TITLE & DESCRIPTION	AUTHOR	✓

Current hyperfixation

Use this list as a brain dump to jot down books, courses, websites, podcasts, apps and videos you want to consume about your latest obsession, so you can find them later.

TOPIC:

- [ ]
- [ ]
- [ ]
- [ ]
- [ ]
- [ ]
- [ ]
- [ ]
- [ ]
- [ ]
- [ ]
- [ ]
- [ ]

Parcel tracker

Missing mail no more! Get the details out of your brain and onto the page so you remember you have an Amazon package (or five!) coming.

PARCEL/ORDER DETAILS	EST. ARRIVAL	✓

New friends

Never awkwardly forget someone's name again. Yay!

NAME	DATE	LOCATION MET	WE TALKED ABOUT...

Goal pressure test

Use this template to assess new goal ideas you have, or re-evaluate existing goals to see whether it's time to cull some.

---

1. GOAL:

---

2. HOW DOES THIS GOAL SERVE ME?

---

3. BEFORE SPENDING MONEY OR COMMITTING, ASK:

- ○ Has this been a persistent goal or dream?
- ○ Have I researched all the associated and hidden costs?
- ○ Is there an opportunity cost (time I could be spending elsewhere)?
- ○ Do I have the money saved for it?
- ○ Have I researched the details (by listening to podcasts, YouTube videos, etc.)?
- ○ Would I be willing to volunteer or do work-experience first?
- ○ Do I know all the worst things about it and still want to do it?
- ○ Do I know someone experienced in this area I could ask advice of?
- ○ Do I have time in my schedule? Can I stop doing something else?
- ○ Does it promote my well-being and empower me?
- ○ What are my support systems?

---

4. WHAT WOULD BE THE COST IF I _DIDN'T_ DO IT?

---

5. AM I GOING TO SAY YES TO THIS NEW GOAL?

Pssst. Check out the Div/Con example on page 121!

Div/Con Planning

1. OUTCOME/GOAL/MY "WHY":

Be descriptive, and visualize how you'll feel.

_____

_____

2. DIVERGENT THINKING BRAINSTORM:

Set a time limit on divergent thinking.

TIME LIMIT!

☐

MINS/HRS

3. MY DECISION:

4. CONVERGENT THINKING TASK LIST:

What practical steps do I need to take that will help me achieve my goal?

☐ _____   ☐ _____

☐ _____   ☐ _____

☐ _____   ☐ _____

☐ _____   ☐ _____

☐ _____

If you get lost and feel tempted to slip back into divergent thinking, remember to focus on your goal, visualize how you want to feel and use that positive feeling to create actionable steps and stay on track. Your future self will thank you.

☐ _____

Div/Con Planning

1. OUTCOME/GOAL/MY "WHY":

Be descriptive, and visualize how you'll feel.

_____

_____

2. DIVERGENT THINKING BRAINSTORM:

Set a time limit on divergent thinking.

TIME LIMIT!

[ ]

MINS/HRS

3. MY DECISION:

4. CONVERGENT THINKING TASK LIST:

What practical steps do I need to take that will help me achieve my goal?

[ ] _____   [ ] _____

[ ] _____   [ ] _____

[ ] _____   [ ] _____

[ ] _____   [ ] _____

[ ] _____

[ ] _____

If you get lost and feel tempted to slip back into divergent thinking, remember to focus on your goal, visualize how you want to feel and use that positive feeling to create actionable steps and stay on track. Your future self will thank you.

Div/Con Planning

1. OUTCOME/GOAL/MY "WHY":

Be descriptive, and
visualize how you'll feel.

_____

_____

2. DIVERGENT THINKING BRAINSTORM:

Set a time limit on
divergent thinking.

3. MY DECISION:

4. CONVERGENT THINKING TASK LIST:

What practical steps do I need to take that will help me achieve my goal?

☐ _____   ☐ _____

☐ _____   ☐ _____

☐ _____   ☐ _____

☐ _____   ☐ _____

☐ _____

☐ _____

If you get lost and feel tempted to slip back into
divergent thinking, remember to focus on your
goal, visualize how you want to feel and use that
positive feeling to create actionable steps and
stay on track. Your future self will thank you.

Get sh*t done days

It's time to tackle some boring but necessary tasks (and reward yourself along the way).

☐ _____

☐ _____

🎉 REWARD TO MYSELF AFTER:

☐ _____

☐ _____

🎉 REWARD TO MYSELF AFTER:

☐ _____

☐ _____

🎉 KNOCK OFF AND RELAX:

Get sh*t done days

It's time to tackle some boring but necessary tasks (and reward yourself along the way).

☐ _____

☐ _____

🎉 REWARD TO MYSELF AFTER:

☐ _____

☐ _____

🎉 REWARD TO MYSELF AFTER:

☐ _____

☐ _____

🎉 KNOCK OFF AND RELAX:

Get sh*t done days

It's time to tackle some boring but necessary tasks (and reward yourself along the way).

☐ _____

☐ _____

🎉 REWARD TO MYSELF AFTER:

☐ _____

☐ _____

🎉 REWARD TO MYSELF AFTER:

☐ _____

☐ _____

🎉 KNOCK OFF AND RELAX:

As we finish this journey together,
I want to remind you of one thing . . .

Your skills and gifts are needed in
this world, and you've got _so much_
to offer. I hope this book has inspired
you to partner with your nervous
system and ADHD brain, and bring
beautiful things into the world.
You're in the driver's seat, and
you've got this!

Acknowledgments

Writing this book has been one of the best experiences of my life, not only because I've loved writing since I could hold a pencil, but because this book has brought me closer to so many excellent people. Birthing this book required me to dig deep and work like a hermit for months on end, which meant I needed my humans (especially those with silly memes) more than ever.

First and foremost, to my husband and creative partner, Eric. This is our book. Your belief in my ideas and ability translated into the most unmatchable 24/7 support, encouragement and loyalty. You know this book wouldn't exist without you. Thanks for bringing meals that were perfectly timed to stave off my post-hyperfocus hanger. Thanks for the 138 pep talks and pillow fights when I needed a good bonk over the head. I love you more.

To my sons, Leo and Oregon. Thank you for your love notes and "kiss storms." Emerging stiff after many weeks deep in writing hyperfocus, I was warmed back to human again by your cuddles.

To my assistant editor, Georgie—my ADHD meme queen. You've been with me on every step of this writing process, from the pink note brainstorm to the late nights on final edits. Thanks for the countless WhatsApp chats and a steady stream of dog GIFs. Thank you for reading every page and being thoughtful, kind and honest with your feedback. This is our #WonkaForFive!

To my incredible literary agent, Jessica Killingley—I'm so unbelievably lucky I stumbled across you, an agent who is not only a force in the publishing world, but who was also diagnosed late with ADHD. You get it. This is just the beginning, and I can't wait to see what we do next!

To my wonderful editors at TarcherPerigee, Marian and Lauren. Thank you for believing not only in this book, but in my voice to share it. You trusted me from day one, and that means so much.

To my parents—thanks for a lifetime of love and support, but particularly that one memorable day at the farm with just the three of us. Your words meant so much to me. (Oh, and I promise I took regular breaks from my hyperfocusing, Mum! Regular-ish . . .)

To my sister, Laura—thanks for the late-night laugh-snorting conversations about hyperfixations and fiddles, and the steady stream of 747 check-in texts to make sure I was eating breakfast.

To Mariane Power, my wonderful colleague and friend. Thank you for writing such a beautiful foreword for the book, for your notes on my chapters and for being one of my biggest cheerleaders.

To my girl, Tara—thank you for being the ultimate hype woman, the long phone calls and making sure I stayed sane during the writing process. I love that our body doubling sessions always turn into long lunches (whoops!).

To Andrea Oerter—thank you for capturing my vision with such gorgeous, striking illustrations on the inside pages and on the cover.

To Ali Rutten—thank you for being my dream graphic designer, and for helping bring my interior layout to life. Thanks for your good humor, patience and attention to detail on the book. I promise this is the final, final, FINAL version!

To Beth—thank you for believing I could write a book years before this project became a reality. Your philosophical late-night voice messages were the distraction I needed.

To those near and far—Gerri, Geoff, Gramps, Ava, Joan, Andrew, Owen, Sam, Sophie, James, Lauren, Chris, Mika, Pete, Arn, Benny, Kristyn, Joe, Ali B, Rob and Amy. Thanks for cheering me on!

To Mohini—my curry queen. Thanks for feeding my food baby so I could birth my book baby, and for taking so much off my plate during those intense writing weeks.

To Cristine—thanks for that hilarious night standing in front of my whiteboard and reading my book outline on sticky notes. That was the first moment it felt real.

To Bernice, Morgan, Tara and Georgie—thank you for contributing your stories to the book. I know so many people will appreciate your words, and feel less alone.

Finally, to my readers, Instagram community, podcast listeners, Future ADHD planner users and all the kids struggling in neuronormative schools and social settings, dreaming of a world where neurodivergence is celebrated, not just tolerated. Find your tribe and be as loud as you can! Thank you for supporting my work and sharing with your friends and family. You're the reason we need to keep pressing forward and co-creating the future of ADHD.

About the author

GRACE KOELMA is an author, ADHD educator (B. Ed.), podcaster and certified breathwork and meditation teacher, with a background in journalism, entrepreneurship and graphic design. She spent the better part of a decade writing for News Corp, designing custom planning tools and globetrotting the world full-time with her young family as a travel photographer.

At the age of 33, Grace was diagnosed with combined-type ADHD, a revelation that changed her life and ignited a passion for researching the intricacies of the nervous system, mindfulness, neural plasticity and their intersection with ADHD. In 2022, after realizing there were unmet needs within the ADHD community, Grace designed a planner grounded in scientific research and tailored specifically to ADHD brains. the Future ADHD planner is loved by more than 70,000 neurodivergents and is now the #1 ADHD planner worldwide.

Grace continues to study ADHD through a range of different lenses, including courses from the Santa Fe Institute for Shame-Based Studies, and studies in Internal Family Systems, self-determination theory, breathwork, meditation and the Polyvagal Theory of nervous system regulation.

Find out more about Grace's work at futureadhd.com.

Notes

p. 9   *Research shows that ADHDers exhibit unique strengths . . .*
- Song, P., Zha, M., Yang, Q., Zhang, Y., Li, X., & Rudan, I. (2021). The prevalence of adult attention-deficit hyperactivity disorder: A global systematic review and meta-analysis. *Journal of Global Health*, 11, 04009.

p. 11   *. . . a world that defines ADHD only in terms of its deficits . . .*
- Bertilsdotter Rosqvist, H., Hultman, L., Österborg Wiklund, S., Nygren, A., Storm, P., & Sandberg, G. (2023). Intensity and variable attention: Counter narrating ADHD, from ADHD deficits to ADHD difference. *British Journal of Social Work*, 53(8), 3647–3664.
- Cortese, S., Sabé, M., Chen, C., Perroud, N., & Solmi, M. (2022). Half a century of research on attention-deficit/hyperactivity disorder: A scientometric study. *Neuroscience & Biobehavioral Reviews*, 140, 104769.

p. 18   *[ADHD] occurs in an estimated 5.9 percent of children and 2.5 percent of adults.*
- Faraone, S. V., Banaschewski, T., Coghill, D., Zheng, Y., et al. (2021). The World Federation of ADHD International Consensus Statement: 208 evidence-based conclusions about the disorder. *Neuroscience & Biobehavioral Reviews*, 128, 789–818.

p. 18   *According to the DSM-5 . . . ADHD is split into three separate presentations . . .*
- American Psychiatric Association. (2013). *Diagnostic and statistical manual of mental disorders* (5th ed.). American Psychiatric Publishing.

p. 19   *A [formal] diagnosis may be validating, help you find support . . .*
- Pawaskar, M., Fridman, M., Grebla, R., & Madhoo, M. (2019). Comparison of quality of life, productivity, functioning and self-esteem in adults diagnosed with ADHD and with symptomatic ADHD. *Journal of Attention Disorders*, 24(1), 136–144.
- Nyström, A., Petersson, K., & Janlöv, A. C. (2020). Being different but striving to seem normal: The lived experiences of people aged 50+ with ADHD. *Issues in Mental Health Nursing*, 41(6), 476–485.

p. 19   *Studies have consistently shown that females are under-diagnosed in childhood . . .*
- Stenner, P., O'Dell, L., & Davies, A. (2019). Adult women and ADHD: On the temporal dimensions of ADHD identities. *Journal of Theory and Social Behavior*, 49, 179–197.
- Hinshaw, S. P. (2021). Looking back on 42 years of research on ADHD in females. Duke Center for Girls and Women with ADHD.
- Attoe, D. E., & Climie, E. A. (2023). Miss. Diagnosis: A systematic review of ADHD in adult women. *Journal of Attention Disorders*, 27(7), 645–657.
- Waite, R. (2010). Women with ADHD: It is an explanation, not the excuse du jour. *Perspectives in Psychiatric Care*, 46, 182–196.

p. 19   *If you've been diagnosed or self-diagnosed late in life, know that it's normal to feel a range of emotions . . .*
- Attoe, D. E., & Climie, E. A. (2023). Miss. Diagnosis: A systematic review of ADHD in adult women. *Journal of Attention Disorders*, 27(7), 645–657.
- Kooij, J. J. S., Huss, M., Asherson, P., Akehurst, R., Beusterien, K., French, A., Sasané, R., & Hodgkins, P. (2012). Distinguishing comorbidity and successful management of adult ADHD. *Journal of Attention Disorders*, 16(5_suppl), 3S–19S.
- Nyström, A., Petersson, K., & Janlöv, A. C. (2020). Being different but striving to seem normal: The lived experiences of people aged 50+ with ADHD. *Issues in Mental Health Nursing*, 41(6), 476–485.

p. 21   *Factors that impact your experience of ADHD include (but aren't limited to) . . .*
- Franke, B. (2023). Editorial: It is time to modernize the concept of ADHD! *Journal of Child Psychology and Psychiatry*, 64(6), 845–847.
- Franke, B., Michelini, G., Asherson, P., et al. (2018). Live fast, die young? A review on the developmental trajectories of ADHD across the lifespan. *European Neuropsychopharmacology: The Journal of the European College of Neuropsychopharmacology*, 28(10), 1059–1088.
- Caye, A., Swanson, J., Thapar, A., Sibley, M., et al. (2016). Life span studies of ADHD-conceptual challenges and predictors of persistence and outcome. *Current Psychiatry Reports*, 18(12), 111.

p. 23   *The concept of neurodiversity is often attributed to autistic Australian sociologist Judy Singer . . .*
- Ortega, F. (2009). The cerebral subject and the challenge of neurodiversity. *BioSocieties*, 4(4), 425–445.
- Baumer, N, & Frueh, J. (2021). What is neurodiversity? *Harvard Health Blog*. https://www.health.harvard.edu/blog/what-is-neurodiversity-202111232645.

p. 23   *Nobel Prize-winning biologist Gerald Edelman . . . Thomas Armstrong, PhD . . .*
- Edelman, G. M., & Tononi, G. (2013). *Consciousness: How matter becomes imagination*. Penguin UK.
- Armstrong, T. (2010). *Neurodiversity: Discovering the extraordinary gifts of autism, ADHD*. Da Capo Lifelong.

p. 23   *Recent studies have investigated societal attitudes and the stigma surrounding ADHD . . .*
- Franke, B. (2023). Editorial: It is time to modernize the concept of ADHD! *Journal of Child Psychology and Psychiatry*, 64(6), 845–847.
- Schrevel, S. J., Dedding, C., van Aken, J. A., & Broerse, J. E. (2016). 'Do I need to become someone else?' A qualitative exploratory study into the experiences and needs of adults with ADHD. *Health Expectations*, 19(1), 39–48.
- Horton-Salway, M., & Davies, A. (2018). ADHD as the Product of Discourse. In *The discourse of ADHD: Perspectives on attention deficit hyperactivity disorder* (pp. 221–252). Palgrave Macmillan.

p. 23   *. . . ADHD is measured by the severity and frequency of these traits . . .*
- Barkley, R. A. (2021). *Taking charge of adult ADHD: Proven strategies to succeed at work, at home, and in relationships*. Guilford Publications.
- Nyström, A., Petersson, K., & Janlöv, A. C. (2020). Being different but striving to seem normal: The lived experiences of people aged 50+ with ADHD. *Issues in Mental Health Nursing*, 41(6), 476–485.

p. 23   *. . . ADHD is linked to a significantly higher lifetime risk of . . .*
- Katzman, M. A., Bilkey, T. S., Chokka, P. R., et al. (2017). Adult ADHD and comorbid disorders: Clinical implications of a dimensional approach. *BMC Psychiatry*, 17, 302.
- Impey, M., & Heun, R. (2012). Completed suicide, ideation and attempt in attention deficit hyperactivity disorder. *Acta Psychiatrica Scandinavica*, 125, 93–102.
- Reale, L., Bartoli, B., Cartabia, M., et al. (2017). Comorbidity prevalence and treatment outcome in children and adolescents with ADHD. *European Child & Adolescent Psychiatry*, 26, 1443–1457.
- Asztély, K., Kopp, S., Gillberg, C., Waern, M., & Bergman, S. (2019). Chronic pain and health-related quality of life in women with autism and/or ADHD: A prospective longitudinal study. *Journal of Pain Research*, 12, 2923–2932.

p. 24   *ADHD challenges*
- Barkley, R. A. (2021). *Taking charge of adult ADHD: Proven strategies to succeed at work, at home, and in relationships*. Guilford Publications.
- American Psychiatric Association. (2013). *Diagnostic and statistical manual of mental disorders* (5th ed.). American Psychiatric Publishing.
- Cortese, S., Sabé, M., Chen, C., Perroud, N., & Solmi, M. (2022). Half a century of research on Attention-Deficit/Hyperactivity Disorder: A scientometric study. *Neuroscience & Biobehavioral Reviews*, 140, 104769.

p. 25   *ADHD strengths*
- American Psychiatric Association. (2013). *Diagnostic and statistical manual of mental disorders* (5th ed.). American Psychiatric Publishing.
- Schippers, L. M., Horstman, L. I., van de Velde, H., Pereira, R. R., Zinkstok, J., Mostert, J. C., Greven, C. U., & Hoogman, M. (2022). A qualitative and quantitative study of self-reported positive characteristics of individuals with ADHD. *Frontiers in Psychiatry*, 13, 922788.
- Boot, N., Nevicka, B., & Baas, M. (2020). Creativity in ADHD: Goal-directed motivation and domain specificity. *Journal of Attention Disorders*, 24(13), 1857–1866.
- Sedgwick, J.A., Merwood, A. & Asherson, P. (2019). The positive aspects of attention deficit hyperactivity disorder: A qualitative investigation of successful adults with ADHD. *Attention deficit and hyperactivity disorders*, 11(3), 241–253.

p. 28   *The past four decades of research on women . . .*
- Hinshaw, S. P. (2021). Looking back on 42 years of research on ADHD in females. Duke Center for Girls and Women with ADHD.
- Stenner, P., O'Dell, L., & Davies, A. (2019). Adult women and ADHD: On the temporal dimensions of ADHD identities. *Journal of Theory and Social Behavior, 49,* 179–197.
- Attoe, D. E., & Climie, E. A. (2023). Miss. Diagnosis: A systematic review of ADHD in adult women. *Journal of Attention Disorders, 27*(7), 645–657.
- Waite, R. (2010). Women with ADHD: It is an explanation, not the excuse du jour. *Perspectives in Psychiatric Care, 46,* 182–196.

p. 29   *Studies show that the rates of unplanned pregnancy . . .*
- Wallin, K., Wallin Lundell, I., Hanberger, L. et al. (2022). Self-experienced sexual and reproductive health in young women with attention deficit hyperactivity disorder: A qualitative interview study. *BMC Women's Health 22,* 289.
- Owens, E. B., & Hinshaw, S. P. (2020). Adolescent mediators of unplanned pregnancy among women with and without childhood ADHD. *Journal of Clinical Child & Adolescent Psychology, 49*(2), 229–238.

p. 31   *"Masking" is essentially covering up your ADHD traits . . .*
- Nyström, A., Petersson, K., & Janlöv, A. C. (2020). Being different but striving to seem normal: The lived experiences of people aged 50+ with ADHD. *Issues in Mental Health Nursing, 41*(6), 476–485.
- Compare, A., Zarbo, C., Shonin, E., Van Gordon, W., & Marconi, C. (2014). Emotional regulation and depression: A potential mediator between heart and mind. *Cardiovascular Psychiatry and Neurology, 2014,* 324374.
- Milioni, A. L. V., Chaim, T. M., Cavallet, M., et al. (2017). High IQ may "mask" the diagnosis of ADHD by compensating for deficits in executive functions in treatment-naïve adults with ADHD. *Journal of Attention Disorders, 21*(6), 455–464.

p. 31   *According to psychotherapist Sari Solden . . .*
- Solden, S., & Frank, M. (2019). *A radical guide for women with ADHD: Embrace neurodiversity live boldly and break through barriers.* New Harbinger Publications.

p. 32   *Research shows that people of all ages with ADHD (specifically untreated ADHD) struggle with notably low self-esteem . . .*
- Cook, J., Knight, E., Hume, I., et al. (2014). The self-esteem of adults diagnosed with attention-deficit/hyperactivity disorder (ADHD): A systematic review of the literature. *ADHD Attention Deficit and Hyperactivity Disorders, 6*(3), 249–268.
- Schrevel, S. J., Dedding, C., van Aken, J. A., & Broerse, J. E. (2016). 'Do I need to become someone else?' A qualitative exploratory study into the experiences and needs of adults with ADHD. *Health Expectations, 19*(1), 39–48.
- Beaton D. M., Sirois, F., & Milne, E. (2022). Experiences of criticism in adults with ADHD: A qualitative study. *PLOS One, 17*(2), e0263366.
- Bisset, M., Winter, L., Middeldorp, C. M., Coghill, D., Zendarski, N., Bellgrove, M. A., & Sciberras, E. (2022). Recent attitudes toward ADHD in the broader community: A systematic review. *Journal of Attention Disorders, 26*(4), 537–548.

p. 33   *Researcher Dr. William Dodson estimates that children with ADHD receive an astounding 20,000 more negative or corrective messages . . .*
- Dodson, W. (2016). Emotional regulation and rejection sensitivity. Children and Adults with ADHD (CHADD). https://chadd.org/attention-article/emotional-regulation-and-rejection-sensitivity.

p. 33   *Dr. Emily Anhalt is a clinical psychologist who spent two years conducting qualitative research on successful adults with ADHD.*
- Anhalt, E. (2016). The trouble with normal: My ADHD the zebra [Video]. TEDx Syracuse University. https://www.youtube.com/watch?v=EAeEQvj16XM.

p. 34   *There are many layers of overlap between ADHD and autistic traits . . .*
- Neff, M. A. ADHD vs. Autism [Venn diagram]. Neurodivergent Insights. https://neurodivergentinsights.com/misdiagnosis-monday/adhd-vs-autism.
- Gargaro, B. A., Rinehart, N. J., Bradshaw, J. L., Tonge, B. J., & Sheppard, D. M. (2011). Autism and ADHD: How far have we come in the comorbidity debate? *Neuroscience & Biobehavioral Reviews*, 35(5), 1081–1088.
- Xi, T., & Wu, J. (2021). A review on the mechanism between different factors and the occurrence of autism and ADHD. *Psychology Research and Behavior Management*, 14, 393–403.

p. 37   *Scientists are confident about the connection between dopamine and ADHD . . .*
- Madras, B. K., Miller, G. M., & Fischman, A. J. (2005). The dopamine transporter and attention-deficit/hyperactivity disorder. *Biological Psychiatry*, 57(11), 1397–1409.
- Sharma, A., & Couture, J. (2014). A review of the pathophysiology, etiology, and treatment of attention-deficit hyperactivity disorder (ADHD). *The Annals of Pharmacotherapy*, 48(2), 209–225.

p. 37   *One broadly cited 2010 meta-analysis . . . theorized that dopamine neurons . . .*
- Bromberg-Martin, E. S., Matsumoto, M., & Hikosaka, O. (2010). Dopamine in motivational control: Rewarding, aversive, and alerting. *Neuron*, 68(5), 815–834.

p. 37   *A 2018 research paper speculated that dopamine may even have the ability to switch . . .*
- Berke J. D. (2018). What does dopamine mean? *Nature Neuroscience*, 21(6), 787–793.

p. 37   *Numerous experiments have also shown that dopamine neurons get excited about . . .*
- Tobler, P. N., Fiorillo, C. D., & Schultz, W. (2005). Adaptive coding of reward value by dopamine neurons. *Science*, 307, 1642–1645.
- Kobayashi, S., & Schultz, W. (2008). Influence of reward delays on responses of dopamine neurons. *The Journal of Neuroscience*, 28, 7837–7846.
- Roesch, M. R., Calu, D. J., & Schoenbaum, G. (2007). Dopamine neurons encode the better option in rats deciding between differently delayed or sized rewards. *Nature Neuroscience*, 10, 1615–1624.
- Fiorillo, C. D., Tobler, P. N., & Schultz, W. (2003). Discrete coding of reward probability and uncertainty by dopamine neurons. *Science*, 299, 1898–1902.
- Satoh, T., Nakai, S., Sato, T., & Kimura, M. (2003). Correlated coding of motivation and outcome of decision by dopamine neurons. *The Journal of Neuroscience*, 23, 9913–9923.

p. 43   *Research over the past two decades suggests a clear relationship between executive dysfunction and emotional dysregulation.*
- Barkley, R. A. (2015). Emotional dysregulation is a core component of ADHD. In R. A. Barkley (Ed.), *Attention-deficit hyperactivity disorder: A handbook for diagnosis and treatment* (pp. 81–115). Guilford Press.
- Retz, W., Stieglitz, R.-D., Corbisiero, S., Retz-Junginger, P., & Rösler, M. (2012). Emotional dysregulation in adult ADHD: What is the empirical evidence? *Expert Review of Neurotherapeutics*, 12(10), 1241–1251.
- Helfer, B., Cooper, R., Bozhilova, N., Maltezos, S., Kuntsi, J., & Asherson, P. (2019). The effects of emotional lability, mind wandering and sleep quality on ADHD symptom severity in adults with ADHD. *European Psychiatry*, 55, 45–51.
- Brown, T. (2002). DSM-IV: ADHD and executive function impairments. *Advanced Studies in Medicine*, 2(25), 910–914.

p. 44   *Research indicates a clear link between how ADHDers feel emotions (more intensely and impulsively) and our nervous system's response.*
- Barkley, R. A., & Fischer, M. (2010). The unique contribution of emotional impulsiveness to impairment in major life activities in hyperactive children as adults. *Journal of the American Academy of Child & Adolescent Psychiatry*, 49(5), 503–513.
- McQuade, J. D., & Breaux, R. P. (2017). Are elevations in ADHD symptoms associated with physiological reactivity and emotion dysregulation in children? *Journal of Abnormal Child Psychology*, 45, 1091–1103.
- Barkley, R. A. (2015). Emotional dysregulation is a core component of ADHD. In R. A. Barkley (Ed.), *Attention-deficit hyperactivity disorder: A handbook for diagnosis and treatment* (pp. 81–115). Guilford Press.

p. 47   *Studies have found that emotional dysregulation in ADHD is a "major contributor to impairment" . . .*
- Rosen, P. J., & Factor, P. I. (2015). Emotional impulsivity and emotional and behavioral difficulties among children with ADHD: An ecological momentary assessment study. *Journal of Attention Disorders, 19*(9), 779–793.
- Schippers, L. M., Horstman, L. I., van de Velde, H., Pereira, R. R., Zinkstok, J., Mostert, J. C., Greven, C. U., & Hoogman, M. (2022). A qualitative and quantitative study of self-reported positive characteristics of individuals with ADHD. *Frontiers in Psychiatry, 13*, 922788.
- Steinberg, E. A., & Drabick, D. A. G. (2015). A developmental psychopathology perspective on ADHD and comorbid conditions: The role of emotion regulation. *Child Psychiatry & Human Development, 46*(6), 951–966.
- Maedgen, J. W., & Carlson, C. L. (2000). Social functioning and emotional regulation in the attention deficit hyperactivity disorder subtypes. *Journal of Clinical Child Psychology, 29*(1), 30–42.
- Christiansen, H., Hirsch, O., Albrecht, B., & Chavanon, M. L. (2019). Attention-deficit/hyperactivity disorder (ADHD) and emotion regulation over the life span. *Current Psychiatry Reports, 21*, 1–11.

p. 51   *The brain's warning system*
- Mirolli, M., Mannella, F., & Baldassarre, G. (2010). The roles of the amygdala in the affective regulation of body, brain, and behaviour. *Connection Science, 22*(3), 215–245.
- Buijs, R. M., & Van Eden, C. G. (2000). The integration of stress by the hypothalamus, amygdala and prefrontal cortex: balance between the autonomic nervous system and the neuroendocrine system. *Progress in Brain Research, 126*, 117–132.
- Jansen, A. S., Van Nguyen, X., Karpitskiy, V., Mettenleiter, T. C., & Loewy, A. D. (1995). Central command neurons of the sympathetic nervous system: basis of the fight-or-flight response. *Science, 270*(5236), 644–646.

p. 51   *. . . people with ADHD experience more life stressors.*
- McEwen, B. S. (1998). Stress, adaptation, and disease: Allostasis and allostatic load. *Annals of the New York Academy of Sciences, 840*(1), 33–44.
- Harpin, V., Mazzone, L., Raynaud, J. P., Kahle, J., & Hodgkins, P. (2016). Long-term outcomes of ADHD: A systematic review of self-esteem and social function. *Journal of Attention Disorders, 20*(4), 295–305.
- Toner, M., O'Donoghue, T., & Houghton, S. (2006). Living in chaos and striving for control: How adults with attention deficit hyperactivity disorder deal with their disorder. *International Journal of Disability, Development and Education, 53*(2), 247–261.

p. 52   *Emotions are energetic messages shooting through our nervous systems . . .*
- Kreibig, S. D. (2010). Autonomic nervous system activity in emotion: A review. *Biological Psychology, 84*(3), 394–421.
- Critchley, H. D., Eccles, J., & Garfinkel, S. N. (2013). Interaction between cognition, emotion, and the autonomic nervous system. In *Handbook of Clinical Neurology* (Vol. 117, pp. 59–77). Elsevier.

p. 55   *. . . the relationship between habits and neural highways . . .*
- Amaya, K. A., & Smith, K. S. (2018). Neurobiology of habit formation. *Current Opinion in Behavioral Sciences, 20*, 145–152.

p. 55   *. . . "neurons that fire together, wire together"*
- Shatz C. J. (1992). The developing brain. *Scientific American, 267*(3), 60–67.
- Keysers, C., & Gazzola, V. (2014). Hebbian learning and predictive mirror neurons for actions, sensations and emotions. *Philosophical Transactions of the Royal Society of London. Series B, Biological sciences, 369*(1644), 20130175.

p. 57   *This filter, called the reticular activating system . . .*
- Hynd, G. W., Voeller, K. K., Hern, K. L., & Marshall, R. M. (1991). Neurobiological basis of attention-deficit hyperactivity disorder (ADHD). *School Psychology Review, 20*(2), 174–186.

p. 57   *. . . prioritize things that align with your interests and beliefs, known as "confirmation bias."*
- Nickerson, R. S. (1998). Confirmation bias: A ubiquitous phenomenon in many guises. *Review of General Psychology, 2*(2), 175–220.

p. 57   *Studies show our brain automatically assesses whether a situation is . . .*
- Korteling, J. E., Brouwer, A. M., & Toet, A. (2018). A neural network framework for cognitive bias. *Frontiers in Psychology*, 9, 1561.
- Berkman E. T. (2018). The neuroscience of goals and behavior change. *Consulting Psychology Journal*, 70(1), 28–44.

p. 62   *Where do our negative assumptions come from?*
- Schrevel, S. J., Dedding, C., van Aken, J. A., & Broerse, J. E. (2016). 'Do I need to become someone else?' A qualitative exploratory study into the experiences and needs of adults with ADHD. *Health Expectations*, 19(1), 39–48.

p. 62   *Internal Family Systems therapy helps you approach that protective part with appreciation . . .*
- Schwartz, R. C., & Morissette, A. (2021). *No bad parts*. Sounds True.

p. 62   *According to perfectionism expert Katherine Morgan Schafler, if a goal isn't reached . . .*
- Schafler, K. M. (2023). *The perfectionist's guide to losing control*. Hachette UK.

p. 63   *Rejection sensitive dysphoria (RSD)*
- Canu, W. H., & Carlson, C. L. (2007). Rejection sensitivity and social outcomes of young adult men with ADHD. *Journal of Attention Disorders*, 10(3), 261–275.
- Beaton, D. M., Sirois, F., & Milne, E. (2022). Experiences of criticism in adults with ADHD: A qualitative study. *PLOS One*, 17(2), e0263366.
- Scharf, M., Oshri, A., Eshkol, V., & Pilowsky, T. (2014). Adolescents' ADHD symptoms and adjustment: The role of attachment and rejection sensitivity. *American Journal of Psychotherapy*, 84(2), 209.
- Dodson, W. (2023, December 20). New insights into rejection-sensitive dysphoria. *ADDitude Magazine*.

p. 70   *The body's nervous system is a complex network . . .*
- Wehrwein, E. A., Orer, H. S., & Barman, S. M. (2016). Overview of the anatomy, physiology, and pharmacology of the autonomic nervous system. *Regulation*, 37(69), 125.
- Buijs, R. M., & Van Eden, C. G. (2000). The integration of stress by the hypothalamus, amygdala and prefrontal cortex: balance between the autonomic nervous system and the neuroendocrine system. *Progress in Brain Research*, 126, 117–132.
- Buchanan, T. W., & Tranel, D. (2009). Central and peripheral nervous system interactions: from mind to brain to body. *International Journal of Psychophysiology*, 72(1), 1–4.

p. 70   *Bottom-up nervous system messages*
- Taylor, A. G., Goehler, L. E., Galper, D. I., Innes, K. E., & Bourguignon, C. (2010). Top-down and bottom-up mechanisms in mind-body medicine: development of an integrative framework for psychophysiological research. *Explore* (New York), 6(1), 29–41.
- Vanderhasselt, M.-A., & Ottaviani, C. (2022). Combining top-down and bottom-up interventions targeting the vagus nerve to increase resilience. *Neuroscience & Biobehavioral Reviews*, 132, 725–729.

p. 72   *Sensory overload occurs when we reach capacity with the amount of stimuli we can take in.*
- Scheydt, S., Müller Staub, M., Frauenfelder, F., Nielsen, G. H., Behrens, J., & Needham, I. (2017). Sensory overload: A concept analysis. *International Journal of Mental Health Nursing*, 26(2), 110–120.
- Emmons, P., & Anderson, L. (2005). *Understanding sensory dysfunction: Learning, development and sensory dysfunction in autism spectrum disorders, ADHD, learning disabilities and bipolar disorder*. Jessica Kingsley Publishers.
- Schulze, M., Lux, S., & Philipsen, A. (2020). Sensory processing in adult ADHD—a systematic review. https://doi.org/10.21203/rs.3.rs-71514/v1.

p. 74   *Research suggests that people with ADHD produce lower levels of dopamine . . .*

- Wu, J., Xiao, H., Sun, H. et al. (2012). Role of dopamine receptors in ADHD: A systematic meta-analysis. *Molecular Neurobiology, 45*(3), 605–620.
- Volkow, N., Wang, G. J., Newcorn, J. et al. (2011). Motivation deficit in ADHD is associated with dysfunction of the dopamine reward pathway. *Molecular Psychiatry* 16, 1147–1154 (2011).
- Tripp, G., & Wickens, J. R. (2009). Neurobiology of ADHD. *Neuropharmacology, 57*(7–8), 579–589.

p. 74   *Author and adventurer Thom Hartmann calls the constant ADHD need for stimulation "the need to feel alive" . . .*

- Hartmann, T. (2016). *Adult ADHD: How to succeed as a hunter in a farmer's world.* Simon and Schuster.

p. 77   *While empirical research on ADHD and interoception is still relatively uncommon, some studies suggest that people with ADHD are less aware of the physical signals and cues in their bodies.*

- Berntson, G. G., Gianaros, P. J., & Tsakiris, M. (2018). Interoception and the autonomic nervous system: Bottom-up meets top-down. In M. Tsakiris & H. De Preester (Eds.), *The interoceptive mind: From homeostasis to awareness (part 1).* Oxford University Press.
- Kutscheidt, K., Dresler, T., Hudak, J., et al. (2019). Interoceptive awareness in patients with attention-deficit/hyperactivity disorder (ADHD). *ADHD Attention Deficit and Hyperactivity Disorders,* 11, 395–401.
- Wiersema, J. R., & Godefroid, E. (2018). Interoceptive awareness in attention deficit hyperactivity disorder. *PLOS One, 13*(10), e0205221.

p. 79   *Psychologist and researcher Nicola Jane Hobbs is one of the leading experts on rest . . .*

- Hobbs, N. (2022). 10 Types of Rest. Adapted with permission from author. https://www.therelaxedwoman.com/.

p. 80   *Researchers have estimated that ADHD children receive 20,000 more negative messages . . .*

- Dodson, W. (2016). Emotional regulation and rejection sensitivity. Children and Adults with ADHD (CHADD). https://chadd.org/attention-article/emotional-regulation-and-rejection-sensitivity.

p. 82   *Intentional breathing . . . can calm us down by getting rid of a stress hormone called cortisol . . .*

- Fincham, G. W., Strauss, C., Montero-Marin, J., & Cavanagh, K. (2023). Effect of breathwork on stress and mental health: A meta-analysis of randomised-controlled trials. *Scientific Reports, 13*(1), 432.
- Perciavalle, V., Blandini, M., Fecarotta, P., Buscemi, A., Di Corrado, D., Bertolo, L., Fichera, F., & Coco, M. (2017). The role of deep breathing on stress. *Neurological Sciences: Official Journal of the Italian Neurological Society and of the Italian Society of Clinical Neurophysiology, 38*(3), 451–458.
- Nestor J. (2020). *Breath: the new science of a lost art.* Riverhead Books.

p. 87   *Psychiatrist William Dodson theorized the concept of an "interest-based nervous system" . . .*

- Dodson, W. (2023, November 6). Secrets of your ADHD brain. *ADDitude Magazine.* https://www.additudemag.com/secrets-of-the-adhd-brain/.

p. 101   *Research shows that in order to motivate ourselves to achieve something . . .*

- Deutsch, R., Smith, K. J., Kordts-Freudinger, R., & Reichardt, R. (2015). How absent negativity relates to affect and motivation: An integrative relief model. *Frontiers in Psychology,* 6, 152.
- Bueno, J., Weinberg, R. S., Fernández-Castro, J., & Capdevila, L. (2008). Emotional and motivational mechanisms mediating the influence of goal setting on endurance athletes' performance. *Psychology of Sport and Exercise, 9*(6), 786–799.